BFI Film Classics

The BFI Film Classics series introduces, interprets and celebrates landmarks of world cinema. Each volume offers an argument for the film's 'classic' status, together with discussion of its production and reception history, its place within a genre or national cinema, an account of its technical and aesthetic importance, and in many cases, the author's personal response to the film.

For a full list of titles in the series, please visit
https://www.bloomsbury.com/uk/series/bfi-film-classics/

T0346847

Xala

James S. Williams

THE BRITISH FILM INSTITUTE
Bloomsbury Publishing Plc
50 Bedford Square, London, WC1B 3DP, UK
1385 Broadway, New York, NY 10018, USA
29 Earlsfort Terrace, Dublin 2, Ireland

BLOOMSBURY is a trademark of Bloomsbury Publishing Plc

First published in Great Britain 2024 by Bloomsbury on behalf of the
British Film Institute
21 Stephen Street, London W1T 1LN
www.bfi.org.uk

The BFI is the lead organisation for film in the UK and the distributor of Lottery funds for film.
Our mission is to ensure that film is central to our cultural life, in particular by supporting and
nurturing the next generation of filmmakers and audiences. We serve a public role which covers
the cultural, creative and economic aspects of film in the UK.

Cover artwork: © Ify Chiejina
Series cover design: Louise Dugdale
Series text design: Ketchup/SE14
Images from *Xala* (Ousmane Sembene, 1974), Filmi Doomireew/Société Nationale de Cinéma;
Bamako (Abderrahmane Sissako, 2006), © Archipel 33/Chinguitty Films/Arte France Cinéma/
Mali Images
Film stills courtesy BFI National Archive

A catalogue record for this book is available from the British Library.

A catalog record for this book is available from the Library of Congress.

ISBN: PB: 978-1-8390-2598-3
        ePDF: 978-1-8390-2600-3
        ePUB: 978-1-8390-2599-0

Produced for Bloomsbury Publishing Plc by Sophie Contento
Printed and bound in India

Contents

Acknowledgments

I would like first to express my warmest thanks to Rebecca Barden, Senior Publisher, Visual Arts, at Bloomsbury, who originally proposed the idea for this book. With her superb editorial guidance and unwavering commitment to the project, she has provided exceptional support at every stage. I am extremely grateful to Sophie Contento, project manager for the pre-press stages of the book, for her tremendous expertise and foresight in obtaining and organising the images. It has been a great pleasure to work with assistant editor Veidehi Hans and her team on the production of the book, notably the art director Louise Dugdale. My special thanks to Ify Chiejina for contributing such beautiful and inspired artwork for the front cover. The identities of the two external readers of the manuscript must necessarily remain unknown, but I record my appreciation for their many insightful comments and suggestions, which proved immensely helpful in preparing the final version. I am grateful also to Professor Paul Julian Smith for generously allowing me to read his volume on *Y tu mamá también* in the BFI Film Classics series ahead of publication in 2022. My thanks also to the School of Humanities at Royal Holloway, University of London, for granting me sabbatical leave to write the book. Finally, on the fiftieth anniversary of the production of *Xala*, I dedicate this book to the living memory of Ousmane Sembene and to the new generation of African film scholars and historians who are helping to (re)discover the boundless treasures of early Black African cinema.

1 Dakar, 1974: The Politics of Setting and Film Production

Dakar, the port and capital city of Senegal located on the Cap-Vert peninsula of the Atlantic coast of West Africa. It's 1974. The country's president, the celebrated poet Léopold Sédar Senghor, has been in power since 1960, the year of independence from France, and has marketed Senegal as Africa's socialist and democratic success story with a fast-modernising economy. Yet the stark reality of postcolonial Senegal is that it has become an import economy with widening disparities in wealth and opportunity. In Dakar, life is becoming ever more polarised: on the one hand a small, wealthy bourgeois elite in thrall to Western goods and flashy status symbols like luxury German cars; on the other a growing subclass experiencing poverty and disenfranchisement. Senghor's regime has promoted a *rentier* class rooted in speculation, and access to government-controlled business opportunities involves rampant corruption and bribery, resulting in numerous bankruptcy scandals. At the same time, under the single-party rule of Senghor's Union Progressiste Sénégalaise (Senegalese Progressive Union; UPS), the authorities have resorted to brutal methods to smother dissent, arresting and torturing dissidents. For example, in 1962, Senghor wrongfully accused his long-time collaborator Mamadou Dia, president of the Senegalese Council, of attempting a coup against him – Dia and his associates were arrested and imprisoned for over ten years. In 1968, when a general strike broke out in Dakar, the police suppressed the popular movement with the aid of French troops.

Senghor's neocolonial embrace of France reached its peak with the state visit of French president Georges Pompidou in February 1971, when roads and buildings on the procession route were hastily renovated in order to conceal the city's poverty. To young radical

activists in the newly formed Movement of Marxist-Leninist Youth
(a grouping that gave birth in December 1974 to the clandestine,
anti-imperialist front, And-Jëf/Mouvement Révolutionnaire pour
la Démocratie Nouvelle [Revolutionary Movement for New
Democracy]), Senghor's zealous courting of the French president was
an open provocation. A student strike resulted in the deportation
and arrest of its leaders in November 1971, including the noted
Niger-born, Marxist intellectual Omar Blondin Diop, who was
subsequently found dead (most probably murdered) in May 1973 in
a jail on Gorée, an island off the coast of Dakar and site of the former
House of Slaves. When the Senegalese state attempted to cover up
the crime, hundreds of young people stormed the capital's streets and
graffitied walls with the message: 'Senghor, assassin. They are killing
your children, wake up. Assassins, Blondin will live on.'

It is against this volatile social and political backdrop of
corruption, concealment and enforcement that *Xala* (1974) was
conceived and produced by the Senegalese director Ousmane
Sembene (1923–2007). With its complex and provocative allegorical
tale of a businessman's sexual crisis within a climate of social
injustice, repression and active resistance, the film speaks to a pivotal
moment of postcolonial turmoil and confusion in 1970s Senegal
when the founding ideals and certainties of independence and
national progress, underpinned by confidence in the commanding

The homeless and
disabled poor in the
shadows of the city's
new towers in *Xala*

strength and authority of masculinity, appeared to be in disarray. Promoted as a mainstream sex comedy, *Xala* was clearly throwing down the gauntlet to Senghor by exposing the fault lines of Senegalese society and the abuse of state power during his presidency. In fact, the film was born directly out of Sembene's longstanding personal, artistic and political antagonism towards Senghor, who regarded the film-maker's Marxist-inspired version of engaged social realism a form of crude populism of little artistic merit. Sembene's previous feature *Emitaï* (1971), about the Vichy government forcibly conscripting men from France's colonies during World War II, was censored in Senegal due to pressure from the French government, which disapproved of its depiction of French colonialism.

With *Xala* Sembene sought deliberately to test Senghorian censorship over what could – and could not – be said about contemporary Senegalese society and state power. Scathingly critical of the nation's blocked social progress, the film expanded many of the key themes of Sembene's earlier work: the gaping extremes between obscene neocolonial wealth and increasing urban poverty; Marxism and equality vs class oppression and corruption; traditional religion, mysticism and folklore vs modernity and change; nationhood within a transnational, pan-African context. Its dramatic opening – the 'revolutionary' creation of a new African-dominated Chambre de Commerce in an unnamed, newly independent African state – was directly inspired by recent events: in 1968, Senegalese businessmen had taken control of the European-dominated Chambre de Commerce, d'Industrie et d'Agriculture de Dakar, transforming it into the African-controlled Chambre de Commerce, d'Industrie et d'Artisanat de la Région du Cap-Vert. This new association was formally inaugurated in January 1970 by Senghor, who cast it in both nationalist and socialist terms ('our socialism, national and democratic, realistic and humanistic at the same time').[1] The building, on the corner of Place de l'Indépendance, Dakar's most important public ceremonial space where independence was declared, is directly visible at the start of the film. In fact, although *Xala* contains only one explicit verbal mention of Dakar (the fleeting glimpse of an entrance sign to the University of Dakar), the city's topography is easily recognisable, from the central business and diplomatic district of Le Plateau with its grand colonial buildings to the Moroccan-style Grand Mosque of Dakar, erected in 1964 as a symbol of independent Senegal and distinguished by its single high minaret.

Sembene had been able to secure financial backing for *Xala*, his fourth feature, due to his national and international renown, which had already attracted the moniker 'Father of African film' (a title he personally never encouraged, in part because it took attention away from the fact that he was also a celebrated novelist). His groundbreaking first film, the short *Borom Sarret/The Wagoner* (1963), made on his return to Senegal after training in 1962 at the Gorky Film Studio in Moscow, is generally recognised as the first film made on the African continent by a Black African film-maker. It was followed by acclaimed longer works such as *La Noire de …/ Black Girl* (1966) and *Mandabi/The Money Order* (1968), his first film in Wolof, Senegal's main indigenous language and *lingua franca*. While Burkina Faso was the institutional centre of African film following the creation in 1969 of the Pan-African Film and Television Festival of Ouagadougou (FESPACO), Senegal – and specifically Dakar – was the epicentre of film production in Sub-Saharan Africa during the 1960s and 1970s. Senghor's government had nationalised the country's distribution circuit in 1972 and, a year later, set up a state-backed production company, the Société Nationale de Cinéma (SNC). A new distribution company, the Société d'Importation, de Distribution et d'Exploitation Cinématographique (SIDEC), was established soon after to regulate the distribution, exhibition and marketing of local and foreign films. One of the first films to benefit from the SNC was *Xala*, shot on the streets of Dakar over five weeks in early 1974. The SNC contributed 60 per cent of the funding, while Sembene's own production company, Filmi Doomireew, provided the remaining 40 per cent.[2] Made for just $130,000, a small budget even then, it was one of six feature films completed in Senegal in 1974, a bumper year for the country's film industry.

Two years in the preparation, and an adaptation by Sembene of his own 1973 novella of the same name (written quickly while seeking to finance the film and based on his initial working script),[3] *Xala* was at once more sophisticated and formally ambitious than Sembene's previous films. Benefitting from a highly experienced crew and producer, namely the film-maker Paulin Soumanou Vieyra who produced Sembene's previous two features (*Mandabi*, *Emitaï*) and had just published the first major study of Sembene's film work,[4] it fully exploited the potential of cinematography and montage to deliver its critique and conspicuously bite the state hand that fed it. In addition, with its satirical comedy ostensibly centred around sex and its cast of strong female characters braving gender hierarchies in a heavily patriarchal society, *Xala* immediately struck a different tone and register from his previous work set in contemporary Dakar, for example, the fictional short *Tauw* (1970), which offered a bleak portrait of the lost new generation, the camera following in bare documentary style an unemployed twenty-year-old man as he succumbs to multiple humiliations (social, personal, familial). Yet despite the new opportunities afforded by state funding for a more extensive production, Sembene still largely adhered in *Xala* to his well-honed, pared-down style influenced by Italian Neorealism and determined by an ethos of resourcefulness, or what he called '*mégotage*' (from the French '*mégot*', the butt of a cigarette), which entailed using leftover scraps of film saved by friends in Europe, borrowing money and employing relatives as crew (his African-American wife Carrie, for example, assisted as secretary on the production). Striving in all his work 'to remain as close as possible to reality and the people',[5] Sembene favoured the use of non-professionals, which, in the case of *Xala*, entailed three months of careful rehearsals (Sembene was a demanding perfectionist committed to collaborative teamwork). There was only one fully established professional actor within the cast, Douta Seck as the

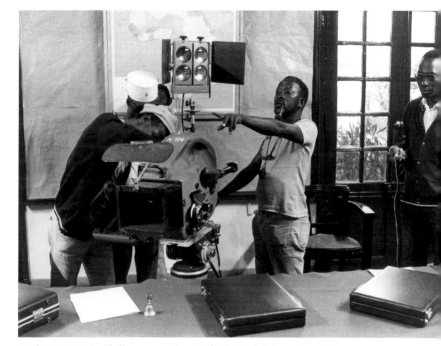

Sembene (centre) with film crew on the set of *Xala* (Michel Renaudeau/Gamma-Rapho via Getty Images)

blind beggar Gorgui Bèye. *Xala* also featured 'real' people, notably Samba Diabaré Samb, a celebrated Senegalese composer and *griot* (West African storyteller, praise singer and poet), and the Star Band de Dakar led by Pape Djibril Fall (though without Youssou N'Dour, who had not yet joined the group).

The extended process of *Xala*'s creation meant that the number of marginal figures was reduced and the original backstories of certain characters omitted. However, the essentially linear central narrative remained the same: El Hadji Abdou Kader Bèye ('El Hadji' is a Muslim honorific denoting venerableness and religious devotion), a fifty-something importer-exporter and member of his country's new African Chamber of Commerce, suddenly finds on the night of his third marriage to a young woman called N'Goné that he is suffering from the *xala* (temporary sexual impotence). He suspects a curse, traditionally viewed as a form of affliction visited upon an individual or clan that has socially transgressed in some way (a sexual curse is often attributed to the jealousy of a first wife).[6] Having bankrupted himself to pay for wedding gifts and a grand reception, El Hadji is obliged to spend yet more money to find a cure from a *marabout* (Muslim holy man). After his impressive ascent from independence activist to trader and member of the Chamber, he will undergo a steep and traumatic decline. He fails to pay the Société Vivrière Nationale (National Food Board) for 100 tonnes of rice, a subsidy which he sells off illegally to his Mauritanian associate, Ahmed Fall, for a quick profit (rice is also a fertility symbol in the Sub-Saharan region).[7] The combined effects of El Hadji's physical condition and corruption result in the collapse of his social prestige and wealth – a form of moral death.

Xala is structured in four parts around the never glimpsed figure of El Hadji's phallus, by turns potent and tumescent: the erection of his manhood cemented by his social success with a third marriage and lavish wedding reception; the imposition of the *xala* and deflation of his social status on his wedding night; the temporary return and re-elevation of his manhood; his ignominious descent leading to the reinstatement of the *xala* and culminating in a final scene of potential redemption. As N. Frank Ukadike writes, Xala's social comedy about one man's desire to regain his manhood is designed to illustrate the simple moral lesson that living beyond one's age and means carries the risk of losing everything. Its eternal themes of greed, selfishness, vanity, hubris and punishment are highly popular in African folktales, as are topics of the lowly rebelling against the powerful.[8] Indeed, Xala comprises elements of the African trickster tale tradition where the protagonist – usually a dishonest individual with antisocial traits – is set a number of challenges with the promise of reward at the end (here, overcoming sexual infirmity). Yet El Hadji also encapsulates the rapacious national bourgeoisie and mercantile elite post-Independence that hides its lack of economic power and dependence on the former colonial power under the cloak of an insatiable lust for Western luxury goods – a tendency analysed most trenchantly by Frantz Fanon in *The Wretched of the Earth* (1961). By exposing El Hadji in forensic detail as a false, corrupt and hypocritical businessman and serial cheat who must turn to traditional remedies to try to lift the *xala* imposed on him by some of the poor he has trodden on to get to the top, *Xala* provides a blistering satire of Africa's leaders and seeks to demystify the power structures of neocolonialism. Its comedy is not limited, however, to the standard features of satire (caricature, exaggeration and distortion, graphic physical detail). Harnessing the resources of popular comedy both to ridicule and exorcise the ideological pretensions and destructiveness of impotent state power, the film operates on a range of comic registers: comedy of manners, bawdy sex comedy (though with little to no sex), pantomime-style farce, visual gags, mockery (of stupidity, hypocrisy, gullibility, narcissism and self-delusion), and caustic parody of the bourgeois elite and its cultural affectations. These aspects go hand in hand with Sembene's strategic use of vulgarity, including earthy humour and crude French words like '*bander*' ('to get it up').

A central aspect of *Xala* is indeed its politics of language and culture, for the downgrading of indigenous languages was a further source of discord in Senegal under Senghor, who had laid claim to a culture-centred vision of national progress which served to obscure his increasing authoritarianism and close ties to France. The country enjoyed one of Africa's best-funded arts and culture systems, enabling Dakar to host the Premier Festival Mondial des Arts Nègres in 1966, yet the official language remained French. It meant that the vast majority of the population – considered by the Westernised, French-speaking elite as rural and backward – remained illiterate. An oppositional political newspaper entitled *Kàddu* ('speech' in Wolof) was founded in December 1971 by the pioneering Senegalese linguist Pathé Diagne with the aim of promoting Wolof as the official national language.[9] The first Senegalese newspaper printed entirely in an African language (it later added Pular, Serer and Mandinka), *Kàddu* formed part of a general movement to reclaim African languages, initiated by students and teachers in Senegal during the mass strike in 1968 when they demanded a reform of the educational system and the Africanisation of the school and university curriculum (this led to the government passing a decree in July 1968 on the transcription of national languages, followed by the creation of La Direction de l'Alphabétisation [Alphabetisation Directorate] in 1970). *Xala* directly targets Senghor's politics of language by referencing this monthly organ, which Sembene actively supported and even helped to edit (one issue featured his translation of the Communist Manifesto). In addition, as a native of Ziguinchor, the chief town in the Casamance region south of the Gambia, Sembene wished with *Xala* to attack the governing regime's politics of land reappropriation through its underlying narrative rooted in the seizure of inherited family land and property. Sembene had personal experience: in 1927, a plot of land in Diéko was originally allocated by administrative order to his people, the Lebus, at the behest of the Senegalese and French political leader Blaise Diagne, the first Black African deputy elected to the French parliament as well as mayor of Dakar. However, the Lebus were subsequently forced to surrender it to Lebanese and French traders, and when Sembene returned from fighting as a *tirailleur sénégalais* in World War II he saw himself condemned to internal exile. In 1970, a series of protests was launched in the Ziguinchor area against the Senegalese 1964 Land Act, which made the state the owner of all lands not formally registered. Casamance was particularly hard hit by this new policy of expropriation, which threatened the inhabitants' spiritual and organic connection to the land and led to mounting calls for separatism during the decade.

However, the force of Sembene's politics of language is often lost in the English version of *Xala*, the title of which – *The Curse* – is already a mistranslation, since '*xala*' is a Wolof cultural idiom for temporary sexual impotence. Moreover, the English subtitles do not distinguish between French and Wolof, hence vital information in the narrative, which features code-switching between the two languages, is withheld from the non-Senegalese viewer, who might already be confused by the representation of local customs, for example, the role of the paternal aunt (or *badiène*) called Yay Bineta, who acts as if N'Goné were her own daughter. (Such loss contrasts with the original novella which, because written and published in French, was intended more for an international Francophone reader, obliging Sembene to explain the names of characters and terms in footnotes.) It means that only those who understand Wolof can fully appreciate how the film's sustained passages of song – composed by Diabaré Samb with lyrics by Sembene incorporating proverbs, popular sayings and metaphors – constitute a crucial political commentary on the action. With its allegory of the lion whose determination, courage and selflessness will triumph over the lizard (a metaphor for the new, autocratic African ruler), the music gathers increasing momentum in the film, culminating in a revolutionary call for disobedience by the wretched of the earth: 'Glory to the people, to the people's rule, to the people's government, which will not be government by a single individual!'[10]

Beyond the usual formal changes engineered in any adaptation, there is a clear shift in political emphasis and scale in *Xala*'s critique: from being merely a polemical denunciation of the French-speaking *comprador* class in the book, to staging an outright attack on the neocolonial political regime in the film. The repeated references to 'le Président' cannot fail to conjure Senghor, especially since the diction and physical stature of the short, bespectacled Président of the Chambre de Commerce (played by Makhourédia Guèye) directly evoke Senghor. In addition, Senghorian discourse is acerbically caricatured in the empty slogans and rhetoric parroted by the members of the Chamber. The film also adds new elements such as the three White European or '*toubab*' advisors who together stand for politics, military force and finance, the key sectors of the neocolonial condition. Other important additions include the petty thief Monsieur Thieli (Wolof for a bird of prey), who transforms himself

into El Hadji's successor in the Chamber by simply buying a fancy
suit with the money he steals from a peasant visitor. The subplot of
this peasant emissary Sérigne (an Islamic honorific in Wolof signifying
Mister) arriving in the capital with the savings of his people to
buy provisions after years of drought (he relates the hardship and
scarcity of food caused by environmental disaster) represents a clear
condemnation of Senghor's failed agricultural policy, aggravated
by the fact that Senegal experienced severe drought in the Sahel
during the 1970s. As such, it forms part of Sembene's permanent
attack on the political and financial class who both exploit and
neglect the peasantry, the most deprived of Senegalese citizens. The
highly theatrical sequence where the peasant emissary is rounded
up and deported, along with the beggars and a student hawker of
Kàddu (another new supplementary figure), highlights the brutal
control exerted by the country's militarised police force, identified in
menacing capitals as the CERBÈRES (after the multi-headed hound
Cerberus guarding the gates of the Underworld in Greek mythology).
Such acute changes in tone and approach from novella to film may
ultimately be accounted for by Sembene's practical need to ensure
funding to produce the film. While developing the initial script
Sembene had to proceed carefully and refrain from attacking the
regime explicitly or risk losing financial aid.[11] Hence, the novella's
less focused and forceful critique was a calculated strategy on
Sembene's part to realise the film on his own terms. Always a canny
operator, he had already begun filming *Xala* without outside support
before eventually securing from the SNC a commitment to contribute
over half the budget.

2 Africanity ≠ Africa: For an African Third Cinema

Xala's extended pre-credits sequence is one of the most extraordinary and explosive in world cinema. A spectacle of neocolonialism in action, it begins *in medias res* and announces a new line of attack and urgency in Sembene's work with its kinetic pace, swift, elliptical cutting (relatively unusual in African films of the period) and fluid use of cinematography. The first shot, a ten-second take and accelerated panning shot, sets the tone. Passing from an extreme close-up of a young man's face, down his red T-shirt towards his hands engaged in drumming, it swerves horizontally to the right and alights on his drum, which fills the screen. That we hear the drumming before we see the instrument establishes from the outset a gap between the visual and the auditory. Cut to a low-angle medium shot of a young, bare-breasted female figure against a blue sky dancing joyfully in a tribal costume decorated with cowrie shells. While clearly situated together in space and time, the two figures are framed separately and as if abstracted from their surroundings. The following, equally short, pan left to right captures a male dancer with an ensemble of four standing musicians furiously drumming. But again, while the sound remains diegetic, the tight framing of the figures divorces them from the larger context due to the limited focal distance. Hence, while one assumes there is a crowd of people dancing and chanting on the streets, the framing and editing of shots create a sense of disorientation, disassociation and uncertainty. Then a sudden cut to a group of eight middle-aged men in colourful, loose West African smocks and sandals, shot at a low angle from the level of a massed crowd of people from whom they detach themselves, and on whom they visually turn their backs, as they rush forwards to ascend the steps of an imposing, neoclassical building. At exactly the same moment, a male voice-off intones in French: 'Monsieur le ministre, …'.

The street sounds continue undimmed as the camera slowly tilts up towards the façade, with the crowd disappearing gradually from the bottom of the frame. A further cut triggers a horizontal pan which traces left to right, in medium close-up, the lettering at the top of the edifice: 'Chambre de Commerce'.

The focus now abruptly changes to the calm sanctity of a boardroom where the eight African intruders have congregated. They seal their immediate assumption of power and control of the Chamber by promptly ejecting the three besuited European men loitering there. As they start stripping the room of its Western ornaments and artefacts, we hear in French the words 'take our destiny in our hands' pronounced solemnly by the same male voice-off. They come out again briefly to place randomly on the steps the assorted signs and symbols of rejected European culture: white plaster busts of Marianne and Marie Antoinette, military boots and a *képi* (or khaki slouch hat). A rapid zoom-in to the Marianne sculpture in the tableau-like arrangement of objects is contrasted with intermittent long shots of the crowd. The camera dips slightly, making the steps appear like the stage of a performance. As the three Europeans hurriedly retrieve the discarded objects as if colonial bric-a-brac, the group of eight briefly hail their fellow Africans in celebration while positioned visually as superior. When they return again inside the building they are miraculously dressed in sharply cut, European-style, three-piece business suits and black shoes. Hence, after initially being immersed in traditional African culture defined by dynamic motion and plurality, the viewer is suddenly confronted – within the blink of an eye – with the stasis and uniformity of a new, neocolonial elite. The sequence is playing out as a Fanonian case study of neocolonialism where there is no real revolution, just a change of skin colour and a moving around of the furniture, leaving the structure itself intact.

Before the new members of the Chamber can get down to business, however, a little more housekeeping needs to be done: the leader of the group, shortly to be identified as the Président, and whose inaugural speech we now realise we have been hearing on the soundtrack, places on a red-cloth-covered plinth where the Marianne bust once stood a black-and-white photograph of himself wearing a tuxedo. The portrait looks as if it might even be that of Senghor, an impression encouraged by the simultaneous reference on the soundtrack to 'father of the nation'. Building to a climax with 'Our independence is complete', suggesting that this apparently spontaneous velvet revolution has been carefully rehearsed and programmed, the Président's stentorian voice continues with a proclamation of 'true' African socialism – terms that directly echo those used by Senghor during the inauguration of the Chambre de Commerce, d'Industrie et d'Artisanat de la Région du Cap-Vert in 1970. In addition to the Président's photograph which we will encounter later on office walls, underlining his influence, a standard Mercator projection of the African continent now replaces the inlaid panel map of the peninsula of Cap-Vert which has been covered up with brown paper. The fictional Président imperiously spells out his real theme – money: 'We are businessmen. It's a victory of the people: the sons of the people lead the people in the interests of the people […] We must take over all the businesses, even the banks.'

The drama of formal tensions and contrasts produced through framing, angles and zooms, abrasive cutting, panning shots and long takes continues when we are taken back inside the building with a high-angle shot of the boardroom in hushed silence. The cross-cutting between interior and exterior conveys the multifarious crowd as amorphous and disconnected, intensified by cutaways to isolated individuals either dancing or playing (a low-angle shot of a bare-breasted woman dancing in front of the crowd, a disembodied close-up of male drumming), and by the general, ambient street noise that sounds as if canned and repeated on a loop – another denaturalising device that further erodes the immediacy of this ostensibly collective moment. Already, of course, the Président's voice was presented as acousmatic sound (i.e. sound without a visible source) before being anchored and identified, only to be promptly re-disembodied.

Hence, at the very moment 'the people' are meant to be united, the film is insisting formally on division and fragmentation in the disjunction between visual space, sound and the human figure.

The new members of the Chamber are now seated triumphantly around what appears to be a blue pool table. Yet in the meantime the three dismissed *toubabs* have immediately returned to the front of the building in a succession of exterior shots. First, a high-angle shot of the more sinister-looking commander in dark sunglasses marching forward into the frame and ordering his military police in khaki uniform and boots to move sharp right and force back the crowd. After the elite's merely performative cleaning out of Western influence minutes before, this aggressive installing of a *cordon sanitaire* around the Chamber represents a concerted purging of the sight – if not the sound – of the indigenous masses. Then the two more bureaucratic-looking figures stride forth, laden with altogether seven sleek, black, leather attaché cases. Cut back in hyper-elliptical fashion to the boardroom viewed again from a high angle as the two *toubabs* stand now behind the new members, their looming presence implying they still call the shots. One European in particular attends like an overseer as he passes round the table to place an attaché case on the desk in front of each member. So now begins a highly ritualised and hierarchised opening of the attaché cases, starting first with a deputy distinguished by his white suit (subsequently identified as Kebe [Abdoulaye Seck]), then a government minister (left unnamed). The highly deliberate nature of this ceremonial process allows us time to count only seven members in the frame, corresponding to the seven attaché cases. Is the eighth lurking perhaps in a blind spot of the image, just out of frame? Even if this were so, he is not made part of the ceremony, since an eighth attaché case is missing. With this subtle yet significant reduction in number, the film is firing an early warning shot to the viewer to beware, nothing is a given here. There will always be some imperfection or hole in the cinematic field, and objects and people can slip in (or out) within the space of a cut.

With the Président's turn now to open his case, our suspicions are confirmed: it is stuffed with bundles of 5,000 CFA (Financial Community of Africa) franc green notes (worth around twenty US dollars in 1974). While the sequence thus far has featured rigorously objective POV shots, there is now a potential subjective POV shot from the perspective of the Président looking intently at his attaché case. The angle is not a perfect eyeline match because slightly lower and square-on with the stash of money, but the next shot is a reverse-field medium shot recording the Président's reaction. His apparent gesture of examining his conscience is exposed as merely going through the motions, however, for within seconds he confirms he is more than happy to accept the bribe, no questions asked. What we are witnessing here is the immediate betrayal and cynical manipulation of revolution and independence: the elite may be cleaning out and discarding the vestiges of their former colonial masters, yet by silently accepting the clean banknotes they are taking everything available in the new nation's coffers for themselves. This highly staged point-of-view encounter with cold cash serves as another warning to the viewer: from this point on we cannot expect to share again the privileged subjective point of view of characters, for that would place us in the same position as these insurgents who, in their acquired sartorial finery, are shown as little more than intermediaries to the former White master rather than the mighty entrepreneurial Black businessmen they aspire to be. Indeed, there is a clear disconnect between their professional pose, bloated rhetoric and extravagant gestures styled on the *métropole*, and the squalid reality and smugness of their corruption as pimped-up fat cats. As Sembene damningly put it in a 1976 interview: 'The people that I show in [*Xala*] are not really bourgeois even if they flatter themselves by identifying with the European bourgeoisie that acts as their model. In fact, they don't belong to any class; [...] these parvenus are [...] just the extreme periphery of imperialism.'[12]

This impression is compounded when the Président introduces one member, El Hadji Abdou Kader Bèye (Thierno Lèye), as a successful businessman marrying for a third time and observing the custom of polygamy. 'Our modernity hasn't caused us to lose our Africanity [*Africanité*],' the Président declares bombastically, to loud applause. 'Long live Africanity!,' the members repeat in chorus when El Hadji invites everyone to a reception where 'nothing will be lacking'. By stating that as a polygamist he is performing a 'duty' in the interests of 'Africanity' (a recent term derived from European anthropology to describe the shared cultural unity existing in African peoples), El Hadji appears misguided, for while polygamy is permitted in the Koran it is not commanded. In fact,

The Président has Dupont-Durand's ear while leading colleagues out of the Chambre de Commerce

the Koran only sanctions polygamy if a man is capable of treating all his wives equally. (El Hadji will fail miserably in this regard and eventually prove unable to provide for his wives and children at all.) Such wilful distortion of religion matches the brazen hypocrisy of the Président's call for an African form of socialism on a human scale. The particular 'epic' Brechtian symbolism of this figuration of national revolution framed in patrilinear terms, whereby those in control seek to appropriate tradition for their own cause, has been well acknowledged by David Murphy[13] – to which one might add that the elite's faux nationalism and perversion of independence, which is hijacking genuine national and social progress before our very eyes, is a façade projected literally from the steps of the Chambre de Commerce onto the local crowd.

As the new members exit the Chambre de Commerce clutching their booty, their number is now magically restored to eight, although the actual number of attaché cases cannot be confirmed. The viewer is offered a graphic tableau of vertical, neocolonial power relations, with the Président in the foreground descending the steps first with his French advisor. The artificiality of this display is highlighted by the fact that the red carpet rolled freely down the steps has become, in the next shot, fixed onto them with brass rods. The servile, largely voiceless presence of the advisor, later identified as Monsieur Dupont-Durand, is a pure sham – a neocolonial mask – since he clearly enjoys ready access to money and power. His loucheness is exacerbated by his sartorial and tonsorial style that already feels a touch *démodé* and a virtual parody of the French colonial image of the 1960s: thick sideburns, moustache, long hair with bald patch, handkerchief dangling from his top pocket and an acutely tight suit. Even his rhyming, double-barrelled and doubly commonplace French surname, 'Dupont-Durand' (a kind of French Everyman), feels a pale imitation of the 'real' thing. With his double-faced pose of boredom and pure Machiavellian cynicism he embodies the relentless preservation of the colonial system.

The eight chauffeured limousines are waiting below, lined up in formation to whisk away each member in an almost obscene display of individual wealth. The second car (a new model black Mercedes) briefly stalls, provoking audible laughter in the crowd, yet this sounds again more like an ironic replay of canned street noise. An overhead shot records in documentary fashion the cavalcade setting off slowly past administrative buildings to the sound of police sirens. Cut all of a sudden to a medium shot of three African women in a private garden dressed in *boubous* with matching head scarves. One is proudly showing off in Wolof her daughter's wedding gifts arranged on small tables: a television set, keys for a car and a box full of gold. The *griotte* (female *griot*) among them appears to ululate her approval of each bridal gift, yet we do not witness her doing this – in another disconnect between sound and image, her punctual shrieks are actually overdubbed. Banknotes are pinned to her *boubou* on which are also printed in duplicate the photographed faces in black and white of an African male figure with short hair and a European woman. They look uncannily like Senghor and his French wife, Colette Hubert, although they could just as easily be two anonymous women, for, as with the picture in the boardroom, the features are left deliberately vague owing to the distance. However, coming immediately after the Senghorian trappings of the Chamber, one is clearly invited again to take this image as that of Senghor.

A parallel female space: traditional and consumerist, secluded and flamboyant

No sooner have we been installed in this domestic space than another mischievous dry cut transports us back into the city centre to witness a second and altogether different cavalcade, photographed overhead in long shot as it circles Dakar's Place de l'Indépendance. This more modest but deafeningly loud procession of white Citroëns includes the new bride N'Goné (Dyella Touré), pictured in close-up behind a white veil during a quick insert where she appears little more than a teenager. At the tail end of this second procession is a truck on which lies perched a blue Fiat 127 Coupé wrapped with red and white ribbons and facing in the opposite direction, instantiating the sequence's formal disunity and mismatching. The general commotion created by this second *défilé* feels like a caricature of the studied pomp of the first (from European 'order' to African 'disorder'). As an intense, full-throated song by a single male voice arrives scorchingly on the soundtrack, the credits start finally to appear in capitals over a series of gently rising, wide-angle overhead shots of the Place de l'Indépendance. Glaring, blood-red lettering introduces a foreboding of danger at the very moment we are borne aloft magisterially in a crane shot over the urban landscape. The chaotic sound becomes more raw and cacophonous: a fiery montage of pained male song in Wolof, intermittent female squalling from the *griotte* and a wall of amplified traffic noise that floods the frame, creating a brute sense of disharmony and tumult rather than synthesis. We are returned to ground level on a different stretch of the road with an unidentified man in a white robe straying as if randomly into view and then walking away from the camera, seemingly indifferent to the wedding parade passing by in the background. This unanchored shot announces one of the film's signatory moves: the merging of an individual entity into a totality (the multitude of the crowd, the flow of traffic). It is followed by a long shot of the Grand Mosque of Dakar, its tall minaret arriving in the centre of the frame as the artfully composed din takes full hold. It is on this charged note of audiovisual friction and discordancy that the prologue sequence eventually ends for the narrative to begin.

Executed with breathtaking aplomb, this supremely stylised and condensed overture, which unfolds like a rite of social observation through a series of demarcated spaces (from policed public areas to enclosed private zones), has consistently stretched the limits of naturalism to portray a topsy-turvy world where illusion, performance, hypocrisy and deceit triumph. The abrupt shifts in speed, rhythm and direction, along with the jolts and dissonances that build towards Eisensteinian impact through ironic juxtaposition, fragmentation and insistent cross-cutting of sounds and images, serve formally to disturb the seamlessness of the elite's rise to power and critically undermine the totalising, propagandistic ambitions of the Président. They also establish in dialectical fashion *Xala*'s defining themes and formal movements as binary oppositions: African tradition and ritual vs European modernity and protocol; individual vs collective; insider vs outsider; centre vs margin; high angle vs low angle; (extreme) close-up vs (far) long shot; shot composition (including tableau effects) vs reportage-style action; the filmic vs photographic; documentary record vs fabulation. Yet there is nothing fixed or stable about these binaries, for within the space of an edit any event or element may flip suddenly into its virtual opposite, and almost immediately flip back again, just as the number of human figures can suddenly change and just as quickly be restored. The sequence thus serves as an initiation into difference and variability, at once visual (the makes and models of cars from BMW to Ford, the assorted rich colours and styles of the crowd) and auditory (variations in types of sound [vocal, instrumental, mechanical], pitch and volume). The structuring principle of such rapidly switching montage, whereby the cut becomes a site of dramatic contrast and potential reversal, is irony and surprise, generating a process of continuous displacement (physical, material, stylistic, generic). Even the predominant French Republican colour scheme of the *tricolore* (decidedly not the green, yellow and red colours of the Senegalese flag) is glimpsed in different configurations, including the photograph of the Président on the red-cloth-covered plinth against a blue background on a white wall.

The multiple divisions between inside and outside, performance and reality, surface and depth forged by this opening sequence propelled Teshome H. Gabriel to promote *Xala* as 'a cinema of wax and gold'. In a landmark 1982 article on African film aesthetics, Gabriel employed an African poetic form called '*sem-enna-worq*' or 'lost wax' process – whereby a goldsmith creates a wax form, casts a clay mould around it, then drains out the wax and pours in molten gold to form the valued object – in order to make a distinction between *Xala*'s external 'wax' (the superficial comedy and sexual metaphor) and its internal 'gold' (the ideological significance).[14] Inspired by Gabriel, many critics have rushed to extract *Xala*'s ideological gold by reducing its complex formal and conceptual challenges to a neat binary: political truth vs aesthetic ornamentation. Certainly, by satirically exposing revolutionary change and independence as pure spectacle and masquerade, *Xala* is clearly inviting the viewer to consider allegorically its tale of an unnamed African country filmed in Dakar as the neocolonial reality of Senegal. Indeed, from the off the audience is instructed in how to decode politically the external signs: the Chamber as the state, the boardroom of trade as corridor of power – all this before we even enter the narrative of the *xala*, an all-too-obvious metaphor for the debility of a false, comprador, neo-bourgeoisie. Such linking of satire and allegory is a common one, for the generalising nature of allegory enables the satirist to incorporate the many aspects and expressions of both the private and public exercise of power.[15]

Yet *Xala*'s tautly choreographed, virtuoso opening is also an ambiguous statement of artistic intent, since it simultaneously calls into question its own status and purpose. If political events are revealed as merely preprogrammed performance (a speech already in progress, the ready replacement of objects, pre-produced photographs), what is the implication of a film that has organised these elements with almost military precision in a tour de force of *mise en scène* and montage? Does the sequence represent a pre-emptive, self-critical commentary by Sembene on the artifice of

Xala, as if he were cautioning the rapt viewer not to be fooled by such cinematic fabrication and to verify every detail? The cultivated slippages in continuity cutting and construction suggest that at any moment the film might slide into doubt and confusion. By the same token, the potential subjective POV shot of money instructs us to see what always lies behind and underneath public display in the political sphere under Western influence (i.e. money), while training us to be hypervigilant and attentive to the cinematic surface.

But can film, even if formally self-aware and ideologically correct in interpellating the viewer as part of the capitalist economy of cinema, fully distinguish itself from pure neocolonial performance (however brilliantly exposed and deconstructed as here) and so become a weapon for social progress? Or is it ultimately doomed to remain a Western apparatus in a global system of production and distribution? Such core questions were, of course, central to the project of Third Cinema during the late 1960s and early 1970s, as theorised by the Argentinian film-makers Fernando Solanas and Octavio Getino,[16] which sought to abandon the structures, values, themes and methods of commercial Western cinema.[17] By the latter was meant both First Cinema (Hollywood) and Second Cinema (European art cinema) and their shared ideological processes of individualism, identification with characters (the obligations of the star system in the case of Hollywood) and continuity editing. In the version of Third Cinema promoted by the Brazilian Cinema Novo director Glauber Rocha, whom Sembene met in Dakar with Vieyra during this formative period, a radically 'imperfect' and 'indigestible' deployment of *mise en scène* and montage that insisted on exteriority opened up new themes directly relevant to the nation's progress and galvanised the people into full consciousness of their situation – the first step to taking collective action.[18]

A key self-critical mode of Third Cinema-style aesthetic and political interrogation in *Xala*'s pre-credits sequence is its explicit intertextual engagement with modernist Second Cinema in the form of the French New Wave, specifically Jean-Luc Godard's *Week-end*

(1967), an apocalyptic account of Western consumer society and cinema (its final intertitle declared the 'end of cinema'). *Week-end*'s multiple rowdy traffic jams (including the celebrated eight-minute tracking shot of a three-quarter mile pile-up) are echoed on the soundtrack of *Xala*, which pits traditional Wolof singing against blasting street noise over views of Dakar's congested roads – part of its sonic drama of competing indigenous, neocolonial and urban rhythms. The soaring crane shot bespeaks the continued economic presence of the French after decolonisation by picking out a Renault dealership at one corner of the Place de l'Indépendance before moving down through Le Plateau past a Mobil petrol station. Yet it also manifests the legacy of the French in the world of African postcolonial film-making due to the expensive technology it entails. For Karen Redrobe Beckman, Sembene develops a dialectical approach to French culture in which references to Godard appear as a form of ambivalent homage, since these same references to contemporary French cinema are integrated into the film's critique of imported Western commodities such as Evian mineral water and Seven Up, the signs of which appear throughout *Xala*.[19]

This represents only the starting point for Sembene's aesthetico-political project in *Xala*, however, for his allegorical mode of social realism, which risks straining under its own weight in illustrating so intensely the blockage of the postcolonial condition, is addressing the viewer as more than just an objective reader of ideological signs in binary formation. In fact, the film's allegorical dimension is arguably not the most original aspect of *Xala*, which continually seeks to destabilise and challenge the viewer by gleefully confounding the binaries it launches, so making it more akin to a postcolonial fable, with the flexibility and porosity the term affords. With its flagrant use of desynchronisation and distancing techniques that disallow psychological identification or visual fascination, *Xala* exemplifies the central paradox of Third Cinema: that formal strategies of alienation can serve precisely to *disalienate* – and therefore mobilise – the viewer. This is Sembene's permanent artistic wager: to make 'free', socially and politically engaged African films within the capitalist system of international commercial cinema and distribution. At this critical moment in the evolution of African film and postcolonial culture during the 1970s, when the forces of state funding, control and censorship are becoming more systematised through preset terms and conditions, Sembene is attempting in *Xala* to forge a new political and ethical pan-African aesthetics and cinematic grammar defined neither by Western ideals, nor by the expectations of the neocolonial elite which slavishly imitates the values and aspirations of the former colonial master.

Hence, having established a clear formal grid in the pre-credits sequence with his sly approximations of First and Second Cinema, where stylistic slickness matches the monstrous display of social and political wealth and excess, Sembene will now complicate proceedings by disturbing *Xala*'s clean, straight lines. It will move in and out of step with smooth Western film grammar and play fast and loose with cinematic form, adopting a more *diagonal* approach and even swerving erratically if necessary, as in the initial subversive play with numbers. The film will even veer off-piste into ambivalence and ambiguity with its constant dispersal of narrative focus and point of view, generic shifts, proliferation of characters and subplots, and extensive engagement with multiple forms of ritual (traditional, cultural, religious, sexual, technical). Indeed, the giddying formalist whirl and overload of the pre-credits sequence may be read as a kind of set-up in all senses, a false sublime of perfection, for what now follows is a more gritty and naturalistic – and purposely imperfect – cinematic style, as Sembene gradually eviscerates the agents of prestige and entitlement in order to focus on those at the very bottom of the social ladder – the subaltern poor and destitute. Put differently, *Xala* will undertake to replace the false self-idealisation and ideological fixity of the neo-bourgeoisie with a new, supple, grassroots, aesthetic approach committed to defamiliarising, demonetising and ultimately dethroning it. Far from being a *clean* counter-hegemonic and merely didactic text, *Xala* will pursue a convulsive, hybrid, metacinematic experiment in contradiction, disjunction, negativity and rupture. It will remain always in transit, restlessly shifting gears between (melo)drama and symbolic tableaux, social realism and metaphor, satire and farce, oral trickster narrative and radical Marxist critique.

3 Defetishising the Fetish

Following the pre-credits sequence *Xala* moves immediately, with no
time for establishing shots, to a series of short scenes of El Hadji at
home, first with his original wife Awa (Seune Samb), then with his
second wife Oumi (Younousse Sèye). He is collecting them in turn in
his chauffeured white Mercedes en route to the wedding reception

which they feel duty-bound to attend. Both domestic scenes bring
El Hadji firmly back down to earth with the tensions of his fraught
polygamous life, to the point he will end up slapping his daughter
Rama (Myriam Nijang) across the face after she accuses him in front
of her mother and brother Moctar (an honorific for older son) of
being a liar like all polygamists. Rama falls down to the floor but
is helped back up by Moctar, who noticeably says nothing. We are
then transported to the reception held in N'Goné's family villa, later
identified on the street by a handwritten sign in French that reads
'Cour du ciel' (literally, Court of the sky) – the elite always prefers
to position itself vertically and high, if not heavenwards.[20] Running
to over twenty minutes, the reception is *Xala*'s longest set-piece
sequence, starting from the arrival of guests to the nuptial bedroom
scene and its abrupt conclusion. By placing it at the beginning and
skipping the wedding, the film is already subverting the standard plot
of classical Western comedy that often culminates in the happy ending
of marriage.[21] More importantly, the reception foregrounds what was
implicit in the opening sequence, namely the status of material objects
(plaster busts, attaché cases, foreign cars) as cultural fetishes, and,
by the way the camera zooms in close to such objects, the fetishistic
potential of cinematic form itself. After showing how the new Black
elite crudely ape the rituals of the former White elite, *Xala* will now
prepare to demystify and defetishise the workings of fetishism which
encapsulates the complex interrelations between inside and outside,
surface and depth, reality and performance.

The Chamber members arriving in unison at the Villa N'Goné
are captured first in an anonymous, disembodying, high-angle long
take that focuses on pairs of polished black shoes moving through a
grey, monochrome, abstract still-frame redolent of black-and-white
German Expressionist silent cinema – as if *Xala* were ironically
referencing fetishising shots of the European bourgeoisie in Second
Cinema to unmask the neo-bourgeois elite. Cut suddenly to a short
insert of people who are already there, looking together off-screen
right. We are not offered a follow-up shot to discover exactly what

they are watching, but it's clear they are waiting outside the garden
gate guarded by security and observing the movements of the elite.
The noisy, celebratory street crowd of the opening sequence has
morphed into this silent band of 'undesirables', the term given
by the police and the elite to the dispossessed whom they dismiss
fascistically as lowlife 'human waste' ('déchets humains'), yet who
render manifest the fractured state of the country as a whole.
Dressed mainly in rags, this group of over fifteen men and boys is
often glimpsed in *Xala* impassively staring into the middle distance
yet rarely heard, except for the sounds of one of their number – a
musician whose allegorical songs excoriating the bourgeoisie and
accompanied by a *xalam* (a traditional string instrument in West
Africa) are heard outside the world of the film.[22] Formally, the
undesirables are shot usually from a low angle, although when the
camera's point of view coincides roughly with theirs, a blind man,
later identified as Gorgui, is viewed more at eye-level, hence singling
him out and granting him a natural authority. When, two minutes
later, El Hadji arrives and grandiosely throws some coins on the
ground for the undesirables to scramble to retrieve, a young boy
within the group is prevented from picking one up by a soldier who
stamps his boot on it before pocketing it himself. Aware of the danger,
the blind man immediately steps back in silence and the others duly
follow suit.

Once planted, the undesirables will forever haunt the frame of
Xala, and, as Marcia Landy suggests, serve as choric commentators
or surrogates for the film-maker.[23] Their penetrating looks as they
watch the preening elite at play oblige the viewer in turn to scrutinise
more closely in a relay of looking. Indeed, what will occur within the
partitioned-off space of the private villa, which only invited, 'clean'
guests are allowed to enter, is subtended – and undermined – by our
visual knowledge of this marginalised underclass waiting indefinitely
outside with their critical gaze. Exactly who these undesirables
are though, and what, if anything, is their real motive for waiting,
constitutes for now a mystery.

The reception is the occasion for a vulgar display of wealth and Frenchified bragging by culturally alienated pariahs speaking the same arrogant, hollow and self-deluding nationalist language. The camera moves assiduously in *cinéma-vérité* fashion from one group of guests to the next. We are made privy to the uneasiness between El Hadji's first and second wives, Awa and Oumi (the latter sporting a tall black wig and sunglasses), as they sit together stiffly on a sofa like outcasts from the hoopla. There is the opportunity also for business. An impromptu encounter takes place in the garden between Kebe and an unnamed businessman who needs a contact in the government to oversee and promote a lucrative dossier on tourism – a clear indictment of a system of government that relies on the West simply to survive post-Independence. Fittingly for the neocolonial elite who abide by imported codes, this brief scene is conveyed in standard First Cinema shot/counter-shot fashion, with the crisp use of close-up serving to expose both men as duplicitous businessmen. Kebe drives a hard deal: 15 per cent and cash only, since he wishes to keep everything *clean* by not leaving traces of his transactions such as cheques – the mark, of course, of dirty business, rather than of 'a businessman's word' as he professes. The pervasive sense of dirtiness and lack of social etiquette in this neocolonialist haven is imparted literally when another male guest, sitting next to his wife, retrieves snot from his nose but doesn't know where to put it.

Another encounter involving Kebe, when he collides with his fellow board member, the unnamed minister, in a doorway of the villa, provokes a sequence of associative editing that exposes simultaneously the power relations within Senegalese society and the ideological grammar of continuity editing inherent in First Cinema. This awkward meeting on the threshold takes the form again of a conventional shot/counter-shot formation as the two strike up polite conversation with strained smiles: 'Monsieur le ministre, after you' / 'No, Monsieur le député, after you' / 'No, Monsieur le ministre, you are the government representative' / 'But you represent the people.' They eventually agree to wait together. In the next shot, accompanied

by the *griotte* and the same woman glimpsed in the pre-credits
sequence (presumably N'Goné's mother), the *badiène* Yay Bineta
(Dieynaba Niang) is cutting up the barbecued meat for the buffet,
followed by a shot of the wedding cake where guests are lining up for
a share. Gabriel rightly argues that the spectacle of two government
officials splitting the nation into halves by claiming they represent
either 'the people' or 'the government' is tantamount to gutting Africa
as if it were a piece of meat where people now assemble to get their
share.[24] Yet the scene also signals a critical reversal of gender roles,
for it is the women who are actively cutting up fresh meat while the
men are merely pussyfooting around.

The reception introduces us to the glaringly casual, internalised
racism of this narcissistic, Europeanised bubble. When asked about
his recent vacation, one Black male guest explains he went to
Switzerland because there are too many 'negroes' in Spain. 'Negritude
really travels,' his fellow male guest avidly agrees, deliberately
perverting the philosophical term for a universal Black identity
and heritage (Sembene, who regarded himself as a pan-African and
'Africaphone' rather than merely Senegalese or Francophone artist,
was a stern critic of Senghor's essentialising notions of *négritude*, as
Xala will prove). All this to the live sounds of the Star Band de Dakar,
playing an instrumental fusion of African and diasporic/Cuban music
– ironic since the band, formed in 1959, had been regarded in Senegal
as a musical expression of national independence. Such commercial,
culturally hybrid, 'tasteful' music for the elite contrasts negatively
with the undesirables' indigenous, sparse and humble *xalam*. When
the Président invites Oumi to dance with him to the music, it is not
only Senghor's vanity and egotism that is being satirised, but also
his cultural and language policies that encourage such fusions. The
culturally compromised tunes – upbeat and unremittingly *lite* – keep
re-emerging during the reception after their first live incarnation, as if
conniving with the various conversations conducted in French.

The reception also lays bare the elite's absurd imitations of
foreign consumer culture and its venal obsession with commodity

accumulation and imported goods presented as a set of brands
(Ford, Mercedes, Evian, Renault, Mobil, Seven Up). The luxury items
are paraded here not merely as the trappings of neocolonialism in
a spectacle proclaiming 'modernity' (the exclusive use of French,
the flaunting of the latest models, modish fusion music, etc.), but
as a manifestation of how objects can become symbolic artefacts
and talismans. When it finally arrives, El Hadji's present of the pale
eggshell-blue Fiat 127 Coupé will remain on the truck, back to front
and gift-wrapped like a giant Easter egg – a commercialised Christian
image of fertility strangely inappropriate to a Muslim wedding
ceremony. A *tricolore* pattern (a virtual default in *Xala*) is formed by
the blue car in its combination of red and white ribbons, matched
by the presentational casket for the car keys: red case, blue top,
white ribbon. Otherwise, the reception is decked out exclusively
in white, with its related Western notions of purity and godliness,
including a six-tiered wedding cake with a plastic model of a White
couple tacked on at the top, which Oumi at one point removes before
tugging at the headdress and plucking off part of its veil. This triggers
a comically hyper-symbolic cluster of edited shots – headdress, gift
casket, wrapped car – suggesting that the real purpose of the inflated
display of wealth is to celebrate in advance El Hadji's breaking of his
bride's hymen.

While the imported car is Sembene's consummate image of
African capitalism and commodity fetishism, the primary fetish
object in *Xala* is arguably N'Goné herself. As Lindsey Green-Simms
writes, her initial appearance while being driven to the reception – a
close-up of her face behind a white veil, lit also to appear of lighter
skin – emphasises that she is a feminised object of exchange, at once
fetishised like other white(ned) commodities and dependent on
others for her value.[25] For Laura Mulvey, who highlights that in the
neocolonial economy the capitalist commodity is 'super-fetishised',
with luxury objects sealing the repression of history, class and
colonial politics under the rhetoric of nationhood, the fetishistic
qualities of the small blue car, for which N'Goné will be paid in

exchange for her virginity, are displaced onto her.[26] Virginity denotes here goods received intact, thus ensuring the groom's prestige, for through N'Goné El Hadji intends to demonstrate both his social dominance and his unassailable virility – the puissance of his penis as phallus (he grossly praises his 'purchase' of N'Goné to the Président and Kebe by stressing her virginal value). When N'Goné finally arrives at the reception, El Hadji removes her veil and kisses her in a display of masculine power, status and entitlement. The fact that he appears as old as her own (absent) father creates an undeniable queasiness for the viewer, although not for El Hadji's guests in the film's narrative. Hence, N'Goné's very image is a fetish evoking the processes of unveiling and disguise necessary for commodity fetishism.

What all the fetishised consumer goods in *Xala* have in common, of course, is not only that they are European and modern, but that they are expensive, exclusive and above all new. Such concentration on the pristine forms part of *Xala*'s core dialectics of hygiene and dirt, poverty and wealth. El Hadji obsessively and ostentatiously drinks only fresh bottles of Evian mineral water because it is imported and 'pure'. He requires his imported car to be regularly cleaned – and its radiator replenished – with the same imported water. Likewise, he will later insist at the bank that the air conditioning be kept on during his meeting, stating that he expects the comforts of modern technology at all times. This underpins his – and the elite's – utter reliance on the West, while also revealing that in the present neocolonial condition water and air have become privatised elements. All must be filtered, mediated and sanitised Western-style, as if shiny imported goods somehow guaranteed immunisation against the omnipresent dirt. Yet human detritus and stench cannot be so easily stemmed or eradicated. El Hadji's secretary and saleswoman, Madame Diouf (Fatim Diagne), fumigates the premises in her constant fight against flies and cockroaches, spraying disinfectant both inside and outside the office to combat the rank smell. Her attempts to cleanse the outside are rendered futile, however – no sooner has she sanitised a bowlful of grey liquid in a drain-cum-pothole in the road where one woman dumps dirty water, than another comes to the same spot with even more dirty, lumpy liquid. Already, in the inner sanctum of Awa's well-kept villa, El Hadji finds his face reflecting back from a conspicuously dirty bathroom mirror (one of the film's many frames-within-a-frame), just before Rama lays into him with the phrase 'Men are all dirty dogs' (dirt: the ultimate insult!). Ironically, the one materially messy circumstance that would be welcomed by El Hadji and his entourage is the trace of N'Goné's hymenal blood to prove his deflowering of a young virgin.

This will never materialise, however, and the whiteness of the nuptial sheets will remain stubbornly intact.

With his Marxist understanding of the fetishistic allure of commoditised things,[27] Sembene works satirically in *Xala* to ensure that the neoliberal dream of a Western lifestyle of clean materiality and mobility is continually blocked, even reversed. Indeed, linked to his wish to exorcise El Hadji's political bad faith and opportunism is a strategy to unwrap the fetishising aura of imported objects and formally disentangle the modes of displacement of the economic onto the psychological, and the political onto the domestic. Yet the visual and oral metaphors of fetishism in *Xala* are also inextricably linked to the central elements of hypocrisy in El Hadji's brand of Africanity, namely religion and polygamy. For alongside modern, Western-style fetishism are the practices of, on the one hand, African fetish worship, and, on the other, animism or *maraboutage*, based around the noble, pre-Islamic figure of the *marabout* folded syncretically into African Islam. During the reception we witness first the role of traditional magic and medicine, starting with the aphrodisiacs offered to El Hadji by his colleagues, including a strong 'native medicine' from Banjul in the Gambia (six pills for instant effect in the sexual 'combat'), which El Hadji grudgingly accepts. However, he aggressively refuses the *badiène*'s exhortation to sit on a mortar and put a pestle between his legs in preparation for the nuptials (a 'ridiculous' custom, he protests), although, as Akin Adesokan notes, this may be due more to a refusal to surrender his manhood to scrutiny.[28] She immediately belittles him with the nasty, racially inflected put-down: 'You're not a White man. You're nothing special.'

Once the *xala* is imposed on El Hadji and sexual impotence rears its head, the second strand of African fetishism comes into play. Desperate to 'cure' the *xala* he will first visit the Président's larger-than-life – and entirely self-promoting – *marabout*, a '*seet-kat*' (generic name for 'soothsayer') fetishised by the Président as 'expensive, really expensive', as if objects and people only count if they possess economic value. The farcical encounter between the two

The Président's *marabout* in mid-performance

is conveyed in shot/counter-shot to denote a purely transactional relation. The all-laughing, all-performing *marabout* uses a material fetish in a parody of the West African practice of divination. The 'magic' accoutrements he hands El Hadji for use in the bedroom include a body wash (holy water), a belt and an amulet to be gripped between his teeth for approaching his wife. By contrast, the second *marabout* Sérigne Mada (Martin Sow), personally recommended by El Hadji's chauffeur Modu (Ilimane Sagna) and located in Modu's village in the Sahel, is presented as a '*facc-kat*' (or 'healer') offering a restrained and literate ritual informed by more recent Islamic knowledge. El Hadji must lie supine covered with a special cloth during the recitation of verses from the Koran. For the narrative of

Xala to work, it is vital that we believe in the supernatural worth of Sérigne Mada (Gorgui will later salute him as 'a man of his word'). Yet by associating El Hadji's costly pursuit of fetishes to cure his *xala* with his material acquisition of wives, houses and cars, Sembene again ridicules the ways in which personal and collective needs and lust for power are concentrated onto objects themselves, endowing them with disproportionate importance.[29] When El Hadji is taken to meet the second *marabout*, first by car, then by cart, with a bottle of Evian water clutched between his legs, the film, as Landy observes, is connecting the fetishism of imported goods with the fetishism of El Hadji's sexuality.[30]

There are two other occasions in the film when conventional African symbols appear in public spaces – not as fetishistic objects or masquerades, but in the form of masks that nevertheless advance the theme of fetishism as distortion. The first is in the Président's office when he is making a call to 'his Excellency' about the shared consequences of El Hadji's financial woes (finance works hand in glove with politics in this rarefied world). In a dense composition, a wooden mask adorns the wall above the Président flanked by Kebe and the minister sitting in the foreground; on his desk can be glimpsed a carved wooden figure kneeling as if in supplication to neocolonial influence (Dupont-Durand is seated off-frame).[31] Together these objects emphasise the sense of estrangement from an African past that is being fetishised by Europeanised Africans. The second instance is the final meeting in the boardroom to decide El Hadji's fate: a Yoruba mask is indiscriminately turned over to serve as a receptacle for ballots. With its face occluded and its normally concealed side made an item of imported bureaucratic procedure, the mask's cultural significance is wholly disregarded. It is now, however, that the theme of fetishism is explicitly formalised. After being denounced by his chief adversary Kebe as a serial scoundrel (Kebe claims that even in the early days when El Hadji performed admirable deeds on behalf of the people, he was already a rogue and his speeches were pure trickery), El Hadji launches an emotional,

Kebe (left) exposing to the Chamber the fetish given to El Hadji (right) by the Président's *marabout*

no-holds-barred attack on his fellow members and their vicious accusations of corruption (a set-piece speech in a public arena is a standard feature of African cinema). He countercharges that the bogus fetish device with its small bell provided by the charlatan *marabout* (sneeringly exposed by Kebe when El Hadji's attaché case is emptied out ingloriously in full view) is far more authentic than the Chamber's 'technical' fetishism. 'My fetish is real,' he declares vituperatively. No matter: El Hadji's attaché case is promptly reassigned to the newly arrived M. Thieli and stuffed with CFA banknotes – a repeat of the opening boardroom ritual in the film's ongoing circulation of Western fetish objects.

How should one connect the various forms of fetishism (traditional, religious, commodity, sexual) brought into play in *Xala*, where the neo-bourgeois elite's European rituals and idealisation of the West exist side by side with the deep, popular belief in superstition and magic? In a 1974 interview, Sembene summarised the contradiction of the elite believing in both modern, technical fetishism and the fetishism of their childhood, including *maraboutage*, resulting in a double dose of bad faith and impotence:

contemporary African society is torn between two types of fetishism: firstly the fetishism of European techniques, and the profound conviction of this privileged class that it can do nothing without Europe's agreement and the advice of its specialists; on the other hand, there is a fetishism of the *marabout*, without whose advice any undertaking is doomed to failure [...] The truth is that this ruling class is as far removed from genuine European techniques as it is from the genuine tradition of African spirituality. European specialists are no more credible than the *marabouts*.[32]

Sembene is suggesting here that the elite's fetishisation of both European commodities and African animist practices has ultimately the same outcome, i.e. impotency, thereby collapsing an apparent binary. Hence, as Adesokan argues, Sembene uses the cultural idiom of *xala* as temporary sexual impotence dialectically in order to spell out the alienation of El Hadji's social class from the genuine values of African *and* European cultures. It is this alienation which produces 'double fetishism' – that is, cultural practice as false consciousness and the contradictions of the import economy.[33]

    To return again to the narrative of *Xala*: the anticipated scene of sexual congress between the new husband and wife on which so much depends, and for which the extended reception sequence serves as a teasing build-up, is summarily elided by a sudden dry cut to the morning after. The twenty-frame shot scene begins with N'Goné ascending the stairs towards the bedroom with the *badiène*, followed in tow by El Hadji. While the latter is associated with the moving image (he is filmed from behind shaving in the bathroom mirror in preparation), the intercutting shot of his bride shows her framed by a duo of professionally made and tastefully erotic black-and-white photographic prints of herself on the walls of the bedroom (a third can be seen hanging in the corridor). These photographs, which serve to emphasise N'Goné's unattainability for El Hadji, are presented as stylised Western artefacts fetishising the African female form and contribute to the film's critique of neocolonialism. A split-screen effect is created across the frame: the photo bust of N'Goné / the back of N'Goné / the *badiène*. When the *badiène* shouts to El Hadji they are ready, he turns the light off on himself, but his eager exit from the bathroom towards the lit bedroom is immediately

interrupted by a false match-on-action cut to the next morning.
The brutalness of this dry cut is offset by the fact that it serves as
a hinge for the juxtaposed shots of one door closing and another
opening – the *badiène*'s friend, the *griotte*, enters the villa through the
garden gate carrying a cockerel for the ritual ceremony of staining the
bed sheets with its blood if there is proof that the bride's hymen was
not broken during her wedding night. The impotent and stationary
El Hadji is now pictured sitting on the bed in abject shame. After the
badiène has verified there is no blood on the sheets, her friend moves
straightaway to slit the neck of the cockerel with a knife, although

N'Goné's movement back into the frame spares the viewer from witnessing visually the slaughter, transmitted instead by the distressed bird's high-pitched sounds of panic.[34]

The unfolding of what John Mowitt neatly terms '"impotent" stasis'[35] continues outside after El Hadji is exiled from the bedroom. As he heads out the front door of the villa into a long shot of the garden, the soundtrack mockingly replays the light, breezy reception music of the Star Band de Dakar (already repetitious with its guitar hook) and snippets of muffled conversation from the day before which now permeate the frame emptied of the distractions of visual detail. In a protracted slow panning shot El Hadji shuffles along sluggishly, his head sagging, past a shrub shorn of vegetation in the middle of the frame, underscoring that he has been denuded of his power. He then stands outside the gate looking forlornly into the headlights of the still ribbon-wrapped Fiat stacked on the truck like a morbid symptom of the neocolonial condition. As Green-Simms writes, El Hadji is looking here at a reflection of his own failure, at once immobilised and feminised like the car itself (*voiture* and *auto* are both gendered female in French).[36] The car's ribbon can only be cut, and the vehicle driven, once the bride's virginity has been confirmed by the breaking of her hymen. Such assurance will always be lacking in *Xala*, and the car becomes before our very eyes a white elephant. Steered into a state of suspended animation, like the other imported cars in *Xala* it symbolises postcolonial impotence, or a temporal impasse, rather than postcolonial modernity.[37] Nevertheless, it is precisely the temporary nature of the *xala* which opens up the narrative possibility that the transgenerational urban space portrayed in the film, where the signs of commodity and spiritual fetishism, socialism and neocolonialism clash and intermingle in such dynamic tension, might also herald potential new forms and confluences of hybridity in the postcolony and point to a positive change in social attitudes and mores, notably around language and gender.

4 The Fading Father, or The Future is Feminist

In an interview with the Tunisian film critic Tahar Cheriaa, where
he explained there was 'nothing pornographic or sleazy' in *Xala*,
Sembene asserted that the film's sexual aspect was only a pretext
for reflection on contemporary Senegalese society and its 'radical
liberation'.[38] African cinema is traditionally discreet about sexual
matters, and Sembene's total avoidance of the sexual act in *Xala*
highlights this in stunningly self-conscious fashion. This is a film
instead about the harsh economics of marriage and the relations
of inequality in the postcolony; there is no time for intimacy or
romance, still less sentimentality. All dialogue relating to sexual
themes is matter-of-fact, even clinical, as when the *griotte* states
perfunctorily to El Hadji: 'You have not had an erection!', or when
N'Goné exclaims: 'I'm still a virgin!' Moreover, despite the constant
mention of the *xala* and blunt allusions to sexual prowess (or lack
of), there is no explicit nudity in *Xala*. The rare flesh on display is
presented in almost casual, non-fetishising fashion: brisk reportage
of the bare breasts of a female street dancer, or when N'Goné is
presented coyly from behind, lying naked and motionless on the bed

A close-up of the
wedding veil on
a mannequin
juxtaposed with a
black-and-white
portrait of N'Goné

after being unclothed by the *badiène*. According to Françoise Pfaff, the erotic content linked specifically to the female body is kept to a minimum in *Xala* so that its symbolic meaning may be increased. Hence, once N'Goné removes her wedding veil, gown and headdress with tiara, they hang from a dressmaker's mannequin like an erotic Afro-European assemblage as if taunting El Hadji.[39] The object takes the place of N'Goné – part of the process of her withdrawal from El Hadji in his decline, for the primary purpose of her union with him was financial support for herself and her family.

Starting with its title designating a man's temporary sexual crisis, *Xala* is, of course, an intrinsically male film. Middle-aged, ersatz businessmen are pitched against another group of men, young and old: the ambulatory band of undesirables – poor and destitute beggars, amputees, peasants and students – located on the margins. This dramatic opposition between two different forms of male homosociality may not be as extreme as it initially appears, since in each case there is a clear leader and chain of command (the Président/the blind beggar Gorgui). How these two figures develop, and the kind of loyalty and friendship they inspire, will be crucial to how one ultimately reads masculinity in the film. The most pressing predicament for maleness, however, is El Hadji's ageing Black body under the severe psychological stress of impotency. As Pfaff notes, male sterility in Africa not only affects a man and his immediate family but also his entire community, since it disrupts the continuity required by his ancestors who might want to come back to earth through his offspring. El Hadji's impotence thus constitutes a metaphysical drama and virtual death.[40] Yet the *xala* is only one aspect of his continually fading condition, for, until the narrative suggests otherwise, Sembene leaves open the possibility that its cause may not actually be the result of another's malevolence, but the effect of polygamy itself.

El Hadji publicly promotes polygamy (or better: polygony, i.e. the marriage of one man to more than one woman) as proof of his potency and Africanity. It is considered a normal perk of success in a patriarchal society where young women are anonymous trophies for older men and subject to the status aspirations of their older female kin – in the case of N'Goné, her mother and her paternal aunt, the *badiène*, who instructs the outwardly submissive N'Goné in tradition: 'Man is the master, you must always be available. Don't raise your voice. Be submissive.' A husband can be expected to satisfy up to four wives sexually and spend three days with each of his wives in turn (a period called *ayé* or *moomé*) in a rotating cycle of allocated days.[41] For El Hadji, who has only a drab warehouse office and the back seat of a chauffeured car to call home,[42] the geographic scattering of his wives, which arouses feelings of envy rather than mutual domestic support that polygamy permitted in its rural context, further adds to his expenses and dilemma while also reducing his authority as a patriarchal figure. He is viewed by all his children except Rama as little more than a source of ready cash, although her brother Moctar at least claims money for school.

In a film so focused on the betrayal of a country by its rulers, El Hadji is effectively betrayed by his own body. We witness the diminution of his virility at close hand, in his every amplified exhalation and aching moan, or when he is witheringly rebuked by the *badiène* for his inability to perform: 'She [N'Goné] came to you [El Hadji] pure and you crumpled like wet paper. Get up and do something!' El Hadji's descent is chronicled in objective, physical detail: from strutting, swanky, debonair member of the Chamber to chastened, ailing warhorse caught in the crosshairs and barely able to walk, let alone talk. Progressively isolated in the frame, desolate and bereft, he cuts a genuinely pathetic figure churning moodily inside. As the *badiène* notes, El Hadji is beginning to smell rotten with age as he sinks ever lower, his face gnarled, his hair visibly greying. The scale of his ebbing powers is rendered graphically: as he prepares the first *marabout*'s wash in the bathroom, his face is reflected in triplicate in the mirror, as if he were at risk of shattering. At such moments of poignant vulnerability one feels a residual human sympathy for El Hadji, for he is himself a victim of the iniquitous

El Hadji reflected in triplicate in the bathroom mirror

system he represents. This does not excuse El Hadji's knee-jerk, physical violence against Rama, however, and, despite everything, he remains a consummate narcissist with an obtuse lack of (self-) awareness and self-analysis. He is in desperate straits yet acts in denial, so vital it is for his sense of identity to have it all and display it (money, property, wives, children). If his social stature depended on his ability to prove his manhood by satisfying two wives sexually and economically, his third wife is contracted merely for the purposes of sexual greed and self-satisfaction. According to Pfaff, African women have traditionally been the custodians and transmitters of African authenticity, and both Africa and N'Goné are fecund, yet El Hadji is unable to 'plough the earth' precisely because he has misused this source of fertility in his drive to validate his social and male ascendancy along Western lines.[43]

In sharp contrast to El Hadji, the role of the women in *Xala* is rich, multifarious and in expansion. First, there are two minor but important characters: the *badiène* Yay Bineta and El Hadji's secretary Mme Diouf. The *badiène* mercilessly manipulates El Hadji by first stroking his outsize ego, before scolding him with the full rasp of her guttural voice as 'neither fish nor fowl' (i.e. a White man in black skin). Mme Diouf is more nuanced. As Adesokan suggests, her independent and unaggressive spirit puts her on a par with El Hadji's Mauritanian trading partner, the merchant Ahmed Fall

Ahmed Fall making
overtures to Mme
Diouf in her office

(Moustapha Touré), for if he is the only man with actual capital,
she is the only working woman in the film, removing her traditional
African dress when in her office to reveal a European-style dress
underneath.[44] Their gossipy flirting, when she addresses him as
Ahmed and stands her ground, confident in French and Wolof,
is clearly well rehearsed. Indeed, his mildly salacious banter and
her complicit smiles, along with her firm entreaties that he desist,
suggest this is a long-running pattern of abusive male behaviour
she has learned to negotiate. His blatant proposal that she take
him as a second husband, just as he already enjoys two wives, is
perhaps the only moment in the film when sexual desire, rather than
need, is articulated. Mme Diouf can also surprise: when she leaves
the warehouse one last time after the business has been dissolved
and reappropriated, she turns to El Hadji and warmly wishes him
'Bonne chance!' before heading off into the crowd. This spontaneous
gesture – a generous expression of goodwill by someone who now
finds herself jobless – is met with uncomprehending silence from El
Hadji. It also comes after the strain of working without payment
while remaining loyal to her boss, the constant humiliation of
having always to correct men like the bailiff who address her as
'Mademoiselle', and the leery disposition of Ahmed Fall. If only the
now diminished El Hadji could match Mme Diouf's natural grace
and stoicism and rise to the occasion.

The film's principal female characters – El Hadji's first two wives Awa and Oumi, and his eldest daughter by his first wife, Rama – are more than appendices to El Hadji, for it is through them that his power is both displayed and negated. On one level they appear simply as symbolic types: Awa stands for traditional Africa, Rama for contemporary Africa, while Oumi reflects a transitional moment in its history. Yet they are clearly delineated in terms of age, class, appearance and demeanour, and together they form a powerful cross-generational female community based on their understanding of mutual differences. Along with its comprehensive dismantling of El Hadji as a new variant of a harmful African male type, *Xala* is asking here whether it is possible to integrate the multiple cross-currents of tradition and modernity in the interests of a more equal, progressive and syncretic society.

Awa's full name, 'Adja Awa Astou', reveals much about her: 'Adja' is an honorific meaning pilgrim (the female equivalent of 'El Hadji'), while 'Awa' signifies Eve, the giver of life (without the Judeo-Christian connotations of temptress) and a model of traditional Senegalese womankind defined by dignity, reserve and loyalty. Her slow, measured, noble bearing comes with being the first wife to El Hadji. She is devout, dresses in the traditional fashion of the older generation (a humbly pale, golden-yellow, patterned *boubou* and hijab), speaks only Wolof and accepts polygamy without dissent, demanding only that her religious, moral and social standing be respected.[45] Biting continuously on chewing sticks that serve as toothbrushes, Awa exudes a reassuring, stable, if slightly pious, motherliness; it is through her that El Hadji recovers his 'Africanness' (she is the only wife he addresses in Wolof). The compromise she makes for emotional and financial security is to submit to the roles and expectations of her sex in Islamic society. She knows that if she were to divorce El Hadji, she would lose the status and privileges conferred on a first wife by Islam. Yet Awa also exploits the rules of a polygamous society to assert her primacy over her husband's second wife, Oumi. When El Hadji asks her on the way to the reception to step out of the car and enter Oumi's house with him, Awa refuses in the name of the same marital laws that force her into submission. She is accused by Oumi of having 'the skin of an old fish', yet when she later leaves the reception her purity is emphasised on the soundtrack by the gentle roar of the wind and sea – one of the many subtle touches crafted in post-production.

Unlike the matriarchal Awa, Oumi N'Doye appears a slightly laughable figure with her brash, flamboyantly European ways and mannerisms. Bare-shouldered and attired in sexually appealing Western fashion (long manicured nails, lipstick, petite black cocktail dress with low neckline, high heels, elaborate wig), flagrantly speaking French to El Hadji and her children while sucking on her sunglasses, Oumi is presented as a caricature of the greedy, pretentious and shallow middle-class European woman. Her villa is garishly furnished in modern, bourgeois fashion, and her children (Mariem, who likewise dresses 'immodestly', and Moctar) are raised in the European style. For Kenneth Harrow, Oumi is played as a domineering, castrating female and mercenary, destructive siren.[46] She talks to El Hadji about nothing else than sex and money in often coarse language, constantly hectoring him about his duties towards her and arrogantly implying that she recognises his authority only inasmuch as he fulfils his sexual role (she makes full use of his restored virility when N'Goné is unable to oblige sexually). Like N'Goné, Oumi quickly deserts El Hadji when he is no longer able to satisfy her sexual demands and provide economic security. However, although a materialistic individual in thrall to the consumer objects she views in high-end fashion magazines, Oumi is also a realist who accepts her husband as a polygamist. The contrast between her and Awa is revealed most strikingly during the reception: while Awa chews her stick with dutiful resignation ('Patience does not kill. If so, I would be dead,' she states wryly), Oumi is barely able to contain her rage and frustration at being made a spectator at her husband's third wedding, especially since her comparative youth might have led her to believe she had a greater chance of permanently ensuring El Hadji's favour.

However, like Awa, Oumi ultimately recognises the need for solidarity, affirming to the *badiène*: 'We women must stand together.'

Rama, who enjoys more frame presence than any other female character in *Xala*, represents an altogether different model of African womanhood and serves as the film's nascent national consciousness. She is deeply attached to her mother Awa yet ready to reject traditional values that threaten to hamper the development of a more inclusive, less polarised, modern African society. According to African tradition, children are not supposed to question their elders, girls even less so than boys. Awa is therefore shocked by her headstrong daughter's impudence in wishing to interrogate her father about his sexual condition. But Rama is her own person: an independent, young, single woman who does not have to grant sexual favours to a man for economic support, as well as an intelligent and articulate militant for Africanisation. Her use of Wolof, which she is learning to transcribe at university, provides the means for cementing her African identity. She refuses to confer on imported goods the same fetishistic quality as her father, and the divorce she advocates is not just that of her mother from her father, but of the country from paternalistic neocolonial rule. The framework for her ideas is illustrated by the posters in her bedroom of historical West African figures: Samory Touré, leader of the Islamic Wassoulou Empire in present-day north and south-eastern Guinea who resisted French colonial rule from 1882 until his capture in 1898; and Amílcar Cabral, the Bissau-Guinean and Cape Verdean socialist intellectual, poet and revolutionary who was assassinated in 1973. Touré and Cabral reflect the continuity of resistance to Western colonialism and embody *Xala*'s message of pan-African class struggle.

Yet while she expresses her opposition to the nation's economic and cultural dependence on France, Rama does not entirely reject French culture. Adopting what is useful for her from European culture, education and modern technology, she straddles comfortably both Western and indigenous influences while acknowledging their often paradoxical nature.[47] Her hair is plaited in traditional African

fashion, not straightened to modern European style, although
she can also adopt a shorter, more practical hairstyle. She rides a
small moped and dons fashionable bell-bottoms one day, brightly
coloured, African patterned *boubous* the next. As Green-Simms
notes, Rama presents a different model of mobility from cars that
are made an object of parody in *Xala* and connote violence (viz.
the traffic accident when the crowd that instantly congregates
appears more interested in the damage done to the car than in the
condition of those hurt). The fact that in the original novella Rama
drives a Fiat, not a moped, suggests that Sembene may have chosen
to establish a link in the film between her and the character Anta
(played by the same actress, Myriam Niang) in the recently released
Touki-Bouki (1973) by Sembene's Senegalese contemporary, Djibril
Diop Mambéty. Anta rides around Dakar on a motorbike adorned
with a zebu skull and horns driven by her lover Mory, performed
not uncoincidentally by Magaye Niang who plays the other (more
negative) representative of the new generation in *Xala*, M. Thieli.[48]
Adopting the same androgynous look, Rama appears to transgress
gender norms and, as Richard Fardon winningly puts it, she remains
in control of her body, her appearance and her life.[49]

Following their initial turbulent encounter at home, the
inevitable confrontation between daughter and father takes place
in his office. This short but pivotal scene begins with Rama arriving
from campus, sporting a short Afro hairstyle and dressed in a bright,
multicoloured *boubou* with colourful beaded necklace. Apart from
the same large earrings, this is a different look from the Western-style
clothes Rama wore earlier at home. There her traditional braids,
full-bodied red shirt and dark grey jumper featuring a white key-
ring design matched the predominant red and black colours of the
bold, joyfully coloured wall tapestry of birds and animals in childlike
patterns hanging on the wall behind her, in a clear rebuttal of the all-
pervasive neocolonial *tricolore* (tellingly, El Hadji physically blocked
the camera's view of Rama sitting under the tapestry before towering
over her intimidatingly and then striking her). Upon seeing her now,

El Hadji reaches instinctively for his wallet, yet by attempting to realign their exchange on a financial basis El Hadji only increases the nature of their disagreement (Rama explains she does not have any financial needs and that her sole concern is her mother whom he neglects). When they try to communicate, they each use language ideologically: he is genuinely puzzled when she replies to him in Wolof and pointedly refuses to drink the imported mineral water he offers her. An Evian bottle sits with him phallically and fetishistically on the table in a commodified two-shot.

The stand-off between father and daughter is determined necessarily at the level of form. Sembene again subverts the shot/counter-shot construction that normally sutures the Western viewer into identification by violating the 180-degree axis rule. Through a series of single shots the two face each other but never match eyelines, thereby giving the impression they are talking past each other and are unable literally to see eye to eye.[50] Such denaturalising of the scene, which ensures that Rama remains as 'other' to the viewer as her father, is extended by the meticulous *mise en scène* featuring two different kinds of map. A medium side-shot shows El Hadji seated at his desk in front of an official map of Africa depicting national frontiers and territories. Rama, meanwhile, is pictured head-on in close-up in front of a handmade design of the continent whose vibrant colours (mauve for the interior; yellow, green and shades of blue for the outline) match almost exactly those of her multistriped *boubou*. In a powerful statement of pan-Africanism, this idiosyncratic representation of the continent is void of all internal boundaries and divisions, and ties the interior space to the exterior through the blanket use of mauve.[51] Hence, while the editing of the scene produces discontinuity, continuity is created between Rama and African culture through textural *mise en scène*.

Contesting El Hadji's motives and behaviour while refusing to be browbeaten by him, Rama acts as her father's conscience. Indeed, El Hadji will eventually learn from Rama about the cultural value and significance of Wolof, although too late (his request during his indictment in the Chamber to speak in authentic Wolof rather than French is dismissed absurdly by Kebe as 'Racist! Sectarian! Reactionary!', while the Président decrees that 'even insults must be said in the purest Francophone tradition'). Yet precisely because of her bilingual and androgynous status Rama remains an inherently complex character who has perplexed critics, notably Mowitt, who argues that she is conflicted in her desire to reject polygamy and French since she is unable to denounce the sexism of polygamy without invoking the language (French) of those like her father who embrace it as a tradition.[52] For Adesokan, ambivalence is central to Rama's personality, and her own fetishes (the moped, colourful costumes, posters of Touré and Cabral as well as Charlie Chaplin) place her in the pluralist, syncretic space towards which the film can at best only gesture.[53] Rama may be the shape of the future and even Sembene's voice, but, as Fardon notes, she has to reject rhetorically all cultural aspects of Western influence, even if that means misrecognising the exotic origins of much of her own brand of modernity.[54] Aaron Mushengyezi questions how believable Rama is as a model female synthesis of African and Western heritage, suggesting that she remains ultimately a romantic (albeit inspiring) vision of a liberated African woman or reinvented 'Mother Africa' (part of *Xala*'s recourse to familiar binary oppositions such as revolutionary 'masculine' women vs villainous, emasculated men, and the decadence of modernity vs the purity of African tradition).[55] This invites a further question: as emblem of a new, modern, feminist, pan-African consciousness, will Rama perhaps initiate some form of alignment with the undesirables whose free-flowing movement and oppositional spirit of plurality and inclusiveness she both shares and embodies? Certainly, Sembene is bringing together thematically marginalised groups – women, students, the poor, the diseased and physically disabled – in terms of class resistance,[56] yet how far is he prepared to take this parallel? Such questions are left hanging when, with the prospect of real dialogue impossible, Rama brings the conversation with her father to a respectful close and leaves of her own accord.

The *homme-femme* in full flow bounding towards the camera

There is another feminine character in *Xala*, however, who also transgresses gender norms and is central to the film's diegesis: the unnamed, gender-fluid figure – a '*góor-jigéen*' in Wolof or '*homme-femme*' in French (literally 'man-woman') – who serves as maître d' at the reception. At one point, when a male guest asks in French how one says '*le weekend*' in English (another telling sign of the elite's stupidity), this tall, imposing, androgynous figure explains '"weekend", c'est "*weekend*"', before turning round and sashaying towards the camera in a sweeping, gold-coloured *boubou* and glowing red lipstick while smiling giddily and declaiming 'S-H-I-T!' in a bold, drawn-out, African-American baritone voice. This defiantly queer statement of sound and colour passes by in the blink of an eye, but such insistence on the lack of difference between English and French – '*weekend*' is a bilingualism neutralised by franglais – clearly expands the film's critique of the French legacy in Africa to that of British imperialism. The reference to '*weekend*' further consolidates the film's intertextual link with Godard's *Week-end*, all the more so since the guest's lecherous chatter with his male friend about offering gifts to his niece squeezed physically between them turns naturally to talk of a Mercedes.

One is tempted to take this translinguistic moment performed by a trans character as another symptom of the decadence and corruption of the emasculated African elite. Indeed, on one level

Sembene is drawing an equation between gender nonconformity (the 'perversion' of perceived African sexual norms) and toxic Western influence (the uncritical use of words imported from the former colonial masters). Yet, as so often with Sembene, such binary equations rarely remain fixed for long, since the trans character is subsequently portrayed as an intimate of N'Goné's mother, the *badiène* and the *griotte*, relaxing and speaking Wolof with all three in the garden. Dressed now in a pale maroon *boubou*, the *homme-femme* proffers an archly self-ironic opinion of the present state of men: 'There are no real men today!' Significantly, the figure is also entrusted to announce N'Goné's divorce from El Hadji by returning the wedding veil and tiara to Awa's villa. When the camera records the figure heading off in a Peugeot with the veil streaming phantom-like from a window, the viewer is accorded time and space in a generously held still-frame to enjoy the moment aesthetically. We see the character next at the villa heading up the path to deliver the headdress and tiara, placed on the mannequin in such a way that it appears penile – part of the film's bulging basket of phalluses. The frontal presence and knowing force of this trans mediator exemplifies Sembene's abiding capacity to confound and keep all notions of identity (sexual, linguistic, spatial) on the move and in potential transformation. In short, the ambivalence that defines Rama and transcends standard tropes of gender proves affirmatively polyvalent through this boundlessly mobile trans character.

5 Resisting the Narrative Curse: Countermoves and Counter-Spaces

When, in his small hut in a remote village in the Sahel, the learned *marabout* Sérigne Mada restores El Hadji's virility, the latter, supine and wearing only a *boubou*, writhes and jerks as if responding to the throb of an instant erection. He appears to be surfacing from a spell, groggily repeating three times 'Modu', to which Modu responds in ritualistic refrain: 'Patron!'. 'Modu, I fell. I'm a man again,' El Hadji declares. The camera catches Modu looking to his left off-frame, as if seeking proof of El Hadji's manhood (withheld from the viewer). After changing back into his regular attire of European dark suit and writing a cheque for services rendered, El Hadji is next seen in close-up in the back seat of his Mercedes, cock-a-hoop and gyrating ecstatically to non-diegetic *mbalax* music (a synthesis of upbeat, Western dance styles with Senegalese drumming). Flush with boyish elation, observed impassively in the rearview mirror by Modu, El Hadji appears to have already forgotten Sérigne Mada's portentous warning upon receiving the cheque: 'Remember: what one hand removes, another can put back!' This is the implacable narrative logic

El Hadji supine as the *marabout* Sérigne Mada recites from the Koran, looked on by Modu

of the curse, a rigid pattern of doubling which El Hadji foolishly believes he has escaped through a vertical manoeuvre (his erection). It is only a matter of time before El Hadji's cheque to Sérigne Mada bounces. Every scene that follows his departure from the *marabout* marks his decline without his knowing it, starting with his return to the city and his second attempt to consummate his marriage at the Villa N'Goné.[57] In her only real utterance in the film, N'Goné explains matter-of-factly to El Hadji, her back to the viewer, that she is menstruating and indisposed.

In *Xala*'s densely packed narrative incorporating multiple subplots, events arrive with ritual inevitability in pairs: two cavalcades, two visits to a *marabout* (one bad, one good), two nights of failed coition (the first elided, the second shown), and so on. Buttressed by the phenomenon of double fetishism, the film doubles down on the reversibility of the *xala* through visual forms of doubling that appear contagious: El Hadji consumes two litres of imported mineral water every day like his Mercedes during its regular clean; the Président is paired with his silent White shadow and retainer, Dupont-Durand. These are spiced with numerous visual double entendres and puns (cutting the ribbon, crumpling like paper, turning the key, driving the car). Such vertigo of repetition can take a spatial form, as when the forlorn bodies of N'Goné and El Hadji are doubled up on N'Goné's bed after their failed consummation –

El Hadji and N'Goné in vertical formation on the bed the morning after

an instance of exhausted verticality within the frame that ironically
contradicts the indifferent courtesan pose N'Goné struck moments
before when glimpsed naked from behind like a '*grande horizontale*',
or high-class prostitute. It serves to confirm what Oumi had said
venomously to El Hadji before the reception while carving a vertical
line in the air with her hand: 'Her [your third wife's] *fente* [split] is
not horizontal, but vertical' – a saucy way of insisting that N'Goné
was like herself and Awa, and therefore no better. The use of '*la fente*'
in the French version of *Xala* renders more explicit what Oumi is
referring to here: the female genital opening.

   Xala's remorseless play with doubling and repetition across
the vertical axis can feel delirious, like the film's restless stockpiling
of vehicles, including Ahmed Fall's pick-up loaded with rice leaving
El Hadji's warehouse – a scene of conveyance replayed as one of
home removals when Oumi, in a rush to beat the bailiffs, hastily
departs with her children in a truck loaded with the consumer goods
provided by El Hadji in wealthier days.[58] Moreover, doubling can
stretch effortlessly to trebling: El Hadji's hat-trick of wives, his face
reflected in the mirror in triplicate, his three ritualised refrains of
'Modu'. Even Sérigne Mada's grave warning to El Hadji is subject
to tripling: he repeats the axiomatic formula word for word
(according to the English subtitles, at least) before El Hadji leaves,
then again during their final confrontation in the city. Like the many
inverted mirror reflections, doubling/trebling and their reversal are
the very motor of irony in *Xala*, to the extent that the process can
appear virtually automatic, starting with the moment in the pre-
credits sequence when the trio of *toubabs* instantly return to the
Chambre de Commerce from where they have just been banished.
Like the fresh, spontaneous music of the reception that segues
inexorably into rehashed non-diegetic sound on repeat, any element
can feed into the endless ironic reversal and recycling of movements,
events, motifs and figures. We witness in hyper-compressed fashion –
the time for a new suit to be made to measure at Chez Mamadou
('tailor to the youth') and topped with a white fedora – M. Thieli's

Instant makeover:
M. Thieli posing
outside the tailor-shop

quick-fire transformation from street thief to El Hadji's eventual replacement in the Chamber.

A more sustained irony of doubling and reversibility showcasing Sembene's intricate method of contrast and ellipsis, disjunction and displacement – whereby the image and soundtrack can operate out of sync and move in different directions – occurs when El Hadji is with Oumi in his office during one of her regular visits for her household allowance. His mind harks back to the previous scene two minutes before, where he attempted to woo N'Goné in the manner prescribed by the Président's *marabout*. The screen takes the viewer back by means of an objective POV shot to his inching on all fours towards the nuptial bed with an amulet between his teeth, like an animal in pursuit of its prey. 'Oumi, please free me. I'll divorce my third wife, I'll give you anything you want, car, villa, holidays in Europe,' he implores desperately on the voiceover, for El Hadji is not speaking directly to Oumi but rather imagining it. The use of an echo-like sonic effect conjures up a fresh sea breeze (mobility for the upper classes invariably translates in *Xala* as an escape from dirt). This mental flashback scene is intensified by subjective fantasy in the present, demonstrated by the fact that the objective shot is not a simple repeat of the bedroom sequence but actually a frontal perspective of the event highlighting more El Hadji's farcical motion towards the bed than N'Goné's

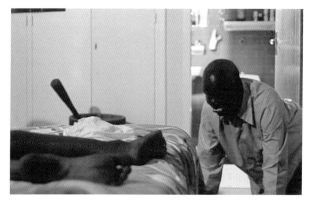

derrière, which previously edged back on the bed in four bursts as she shrieked in fear. Further formal irony is generated by the knowledge that the original event was presented as a flash-forward in two parts, corresponding to the two stages of El Hadji's preparation for coition (washing and crawling). Oumi soon snaps him out of his reverie by metacinematically clapping her hands in his face like a clapperboard.

The most dramatic instance of ironic doubling and reversal in *Xala* is El Hadji's second downfall due to economic impotency. This fall is more lethal than the sexual breakdown that precipitated it because the stakes are now even greater: after excessive expenditure (the costly marriage reception and presents, payments to restore his manhood) he is now depleted of funds and bankrupt, resulting in a total loss of social status and power. Indeed, a vertical ascent of such cocksure ambition as El Hadji's can only be followed in *Xala* by an equally precipitous descent to the murky depths. The narrative process of his unravelling runs through in reverse the earlier stages of his journey in a *mise en abyme* of repetition, captured in graphic fashion in the lift he takes after leaving the Président's office on the way to visit his 'cuz' (Farba Sarr), the assistant director of his bank, to request a loan. The collapse takes a full seventeen seconds and is framed by the scene of the Président calling the banker and the latter receiving his order of denial.[59] El Hadji's entry into the lift is recorded via its large interior mirror. The shot is set up so that only the front of his left shoulder, and the left side of his head and left ear, are visible in the left foreground (his face is elided), while in the background reflection occupying nearly two thirds of the frame can be glimpsed the right half of his upper torso and the right of his head and right ear from behind (with slightly more of his head and hair). This is a pure optical effect of mirror reflection, for only half of his body is actually in shot: the inverted doubling in the mirror causes his left front side to appear as if it were his right back side. The viewer is thus offered a view of El Hadji he could not enjoy himself were he to look in the mirror. This asymmetrical

Going down: El Hadji doubled and inverted by his reflection in the lift mirror

juxtaposition of real body and mirrored image creates a double figure intersected by a line formed by the edge of the mirror. In what is effectively a form of montage by means of *mise en scène*, the integrity of El Hadji's body appears as if severed by the framing, revealing a fracture in his very identity – the entirely logical consequence of a film where mirror shots have been used extensively to reflect the new Black neo-bourgeoisie mirroring themselves narcissistically on the European ruling class. As Harrow suggests, this doubled image, belonging not entirely to the spaces of reflected or mimetic reality, conveys the liminal aspect of the trickster whose real visage does not belong to either realm but falls somewhere between the two. El Hadji stands doubly split, visually a partial being with bits and pieces of a man divided against himself, at the very moment he thinks himself cured and whole.[60] He is now in freefall, with events spiralling out of control. This systematic breakdown is registered floor by floor – the time it takes for the Président to phone the bank with the message that will out-trick him. And just as doubling breeds doubling, so amputation generates amputation, for the shot immediately following – a full-frame image of abstract latticework of horizontal and vertical lines on the concrete façade of the administrative building – introduces another kind of dismemberment: the name of the bank, the Banque Centrale Internationale pour l'Afrique Occidentale (BCIAO), is reduced by the cropped frame to 'Internationale pour l'Afrique Occidentale'.

Such intense scenes of narrative doubling/trebling and vertical reversal across multiple planes throw into powerful relief what Sembene is ultimately aiming to achieve in *Xala*, namely an audiovisual economy that breaks away from the false idealism and vertical ideology of both neocolonialism and First Cinema towards a more direct and dynamic 'horizontal' engagement with the social totality depicted. This pivots on the lateral movements and counter-spaces set in motion by the subclass of undesirables who are continually on the move and defy fixed settings. The loose, roving band of men and boys survive by living off the cast-offs of the

wealthy in the rich streets of the centre (their preferred site is outside
El Hadji's office where they are always already waiting), and for this
reason they are associated with material dirt (allusions to rubbish
routinely prefigure their appearance). Put another way, they are
the bourgeoisie's byproducts and leftovers subsumed like a caste of
untouchables into the urban backdrop of waste and pollution.[61] They
are not homogenous, however, but rather an unquantifiable, motley
crew incorporating beggars, cripples and amputees, plus anyone
else who wishes to join. Indeed, they are continually expanding
through force of circumstances, adding to their number the young
Kàddu seller and the robbed peasant emissary who are rounded
up indiscriminately at the same time by the CERBÈRES led by the
police commander Matt (short for Matthieu). Moreover, they do not
conform to a set sartorial pattern like the phoney businessmen in
their uniform suits and attaché cases. Their multifarious style of dress
– an array of dishevelled and cobbled-together secondhand garments
and rags – emphasises their uncontainable, impure eclecticism (one
wears an American college football shirt reflecting the percolation of
Western consumer goods at every level of postcolonial society).

When El Hadji lets rip at the Chamber following his ugly
dismissal, he expresses what the viewer already knows: that the
real dirt in the city stems not from the undesirables but from the
entirely self-regarding, complacent and morally unclean elite. With
their dog-eat-dog shenanigans and conspicuous consumption, the
Chamber members are the city's real parasites and thieves, laying
waste to society and the environment with their profligate behaviour,
encapsulated by the parade of individual luxury limousines. Even
Modu as loyal chauffeur to the elite routinely discards empty
Evian bottles onto the street during the cleaning of his master's
white Mercedes. That the screen time taken by Modu to fill with
water both the car radiator and a blue bucket corresponds to the
time these actions would take in reality only underlines the sense
of wastefulness. Moreover, Modu employs for the job one of the
young undesirables beaten by a police baton, his forehead covered

with plasters, demonstrating that Modu can also act like his boss in a spiral of exploitation. By contrast, the physically unclean undesirables maintain their integrity and neither steal nor create waste. Instead, they share collectively all they acquire, from food to secondhand clothes which they recycle – a pioneering instance of eco-sustainability in African cinema that accords with Sembene's own practice of *mégotage*. Indeed, in the face of a punitive, militarised, biopolitical regime, they uphold a relational ethics of care and support grounded in mutuality. At the open-air food shack where they make an impromptu pit stop, the camera focuses on each equally, concentrating in close-up on the tactility of their hands as they pass among themselves bread and instant coffee while exchanging common feelings of loss, anger and frustration. The communal ceremony complete, Gorgui pays for everyone, stating that they owe nothing to anybody ('We have no bills').

The countervailing influence and comportment of the undesirables generates its own formal countermoves. They are the embodiment of horizontality in *Xala*, for, in marked contrast to the film's fetishising vertical and high-angle shots, particularising close-ups and zoomings-in associated with the hierarchical elite (the use of a high angle to record the police round-up is a notable case in point), they are portrayed in wide-angle shots creating horizontal and diagonal lines of passage across the screen, usually in a still-frame or gentle panning long shot to register the flow of movement.[62] This honours Third Cinema's priority of space over time, hence long takes, but also, as Gabriel notes, a 'preponderance of wide-angle shots of longer duration [which] deal with a viewer's sense of community and how people fit in nature'.[63] Moreover, the various members of the group are not singled out individually by the camera but rather embraced in their communal movement. If they are occasionally pictured alone on the streets, it is always from a respectful distance as they move to rejoin the others.

In short, the undesirables are the means for Sembene to break out of the fatal logic and narrative grid of doubling and reversal

and resignify cinematic space – the first stage in the process
of charting new African coordinates in Third Cinema. Their
proliferating movement across the cityscape generates an open
frame – let us call it a new, liminal, Third Space. An exemplary
instance is when they make their way back to the city from its far-
flung fringes where they have been unceremoniously dumped by
the police after being forcibly removed on the grounds they are a
threat to tourism (the neocolonial city must be kept clean for rich
Westerners). Despite their bodily impairments and the effects of
disease, compounded by injuries inflicted by the authorities, they
steadfastly traverse the stifling, barren Sahel landscape in a succession
of long shots, from static to slow panning shots. The amputees,
some on crutches, some with legs shrivelled by polio, crawl with
their hands or drag themselves along on their knees, while the most
disabled are carried. Their framing in pairs and groups through
wide-frame shots accentuates their collective agency, willpower and
exuberant kinship in disability. Such an unstoppable surge of energy
creates within the cinematic frame new, ad hoc visual configurations
between the male figures as well as with the natural elements (the
searing expanse of sand, the cloudless blue sky) – part of Sembene's
strategy of clearing the ground for more fluid, irregular types of
relational and aesthetic space. The sense of an expanding, epic
frame, and of a mobile homosocial space, is intensified by the
emotive chanting of the singer-musician, whose stirring song about
the noble lion and the lizard, set to the tune of his wailing *xalam*,
resounds in the frame. It is a piercing statement of revolt, first heard
during the wedding reception where it insinuated itself among the
jarring noises of the ministerial entourage and the *griotte* praising
the worthy lines of descent of the bride and groom. At such moments
as this, when the lyrical resonates so compulsively with the spatial
and music dilates the frame, Sembene reveals he has far more in
common with his contemporary Mambéty, with whom he is routinely
contrasted on the grounds of Mambéty's highly poetic style and
politically non-aligned approach.

When the undesirables arrive back in the city, proceeding from right to left across the highway, the camera opens up gently with a slow zoom-out. Significantly, the street sign 'Soyez les bienvenus' ('Welcome') moves slowly out of focus as a zoom-out opens up to embrace them in their surroundings. The tops of the concrete towers in the far background appear all but insignificant because only half-visible behind the shacks and trees in the foreground. Hence, it is not just that the resolute return of the undesirables constitutes a return of the elite's repressed, and specifically El Hadji's repressed (we recall that El Hadji's appeal to the Président to deport them was in response to the latter enquiring who caused the xala, prompting El Hadji to close his warehouse window to keep out the chanting of the singer-musician preaching action – an involuntary acknowledgment of a certain truth and El Hadji's immediate need to re-enact its repression[64]). More affirmatively, the undesirables are redefining the parameters of social space and lived experience on their own terms, establishing a new cartography of displacement in an open, free, mobile frame sealed by the camera's demotion of the French street sign.

If the undesirables and their sideways motion personify the ethos of horizontality in *Xala*, crucially they do not own it, for it is dispersed formally and felt differently across a range of levels that exceed the common bounds of dramatic narrative and genre. Indeed, *Xala*'s poetic, horizontalising acts of cinema testify to Sembene's injunction not to pander to First Cinema's expectations of visual spectacle and to dedramatise the event, even to the point of its omission (the abortive act of sexual consummation, the traffic accident). Yet it is also precisely to prevent *Xala*'s well-oiled structural machine from appearing too slick, too didactically tight, and thus itself a form of neo-bourgeois polish, that Sembene diversifies and muddies the format by moving in and out of genre without notice and administering decisive ruptures to cinematic grammar. Just as there are odd gaps and ironic openings in the narrative, so, too, on the film's surface, moments of confusion and

opacity arise in the cinematography and montage that eschew
easy legibility and appear more playful and less programmed, even
arbitrary, as if outstripping Sembene's firm authorial control and
stylistic design – part of his artistic bid to keep the film moving in the
very image of the undesirables. Such formal moves, which can appear
superfluous because disconnected from the immediate demands of
the narrative, might be regarded as the film's own internal, ethical
means of self-resistance, for *Xala* consistently undermines its
own drive towards knowledge and certainty through strategies of
ambivalence, differentiation and discontinuity, in turn complicating
any over-neat opposition between the vertical and horizontal. Indeed,
shocks and aberrations in form, together with marks of imperfection,
illustrate Sembene's impressive commitment to creating space for the
unforeseen and spontaneous, the marginal and everyday, even doubt
and error – in a word, difference.

Take, for example, the scene of the repossession of El Hadji's
business by the Société Vivrière Nationale and the confiscation of
his Mercedes. El Hadji appears disoriented and unable to speak. In
a delicate play of magnified volume and pitch, he groans audibly in
self-deflation as he sits down on his sole remaining possession – a
bare wooden stool that appears 'a shrunken, or wizened version of
the proud object of display'.[65] None of the three soldiers serving as
witnesses knows how to drive – a farcical state of affairs proposed
as a sign of their own alienation. Hence, they have to push the car
together physically in an extraordinary case of triple male shunting.
We behold full-on their pert posteriors in lateral series as they propel
the car forward, with the *maître* (bailiff) still inside, in the direction
of the Grand Mosque of Dakar visible in the far background. The
camera appears drawn magnetically to its minaret whose phallicity
has been latent up until now, in part because it has not been revealed
in its entirety, including the metal cone and jamour (or finial)
with gilded copper balls at the apex. A rapid and direct vertical
zoom-in towards the knob-like shape at the top carries a tangible
erotic charge and contributes to what might justly be called, in

view of the exclusively male context of tightly stacked *derrières* in the foreground, a homoerotics of the gaze. The sexual act may be conspicuous by its absence in *Xala*, but that still leaves room for the associative free-play of the erotic which swells the frame here in its very ambiguity.

There are other loose and apparently random moments of form and style in *Xala*, such as the sudden switch to a handheld, shoulder high, mobile camera when we enter Rama's bedroom behind Awa, and at an exceptionally slow and awkward pace – as if Sembene were creating formal friction with the viewer in advance of the uncomfortable conversation between mother and daughter about communicating with El Hadji. This denaturalising technique allows us time to register the posters on Rama's walls one by one (Touré, Cabral, Chaplin). The fact that the camera is tracing an imperfect horizontal line serves to place Rama in formal parallel with the undesirables. Her identification with horizontality, as well as mobility, had been signalled in her first scene in Awa's villa by means of a slow, lateral, left tracking shot behind the back of Awa as the latter talked to Rama directly facing her. Such staged camera movement in a space that, with African masks and artefacts, denotes authenticity formally established a new type of motion in the film. Rama will henceforth be identified with horizontality contra the verticality of her father. However, despite their formal linking, Sembene will ultimately refrain from smoothing out the film's various expressions of oppositionality with an overdetermined, quick-fix, political alliance between Rama and the undesirables.

An equally swift, unexplained, shoulder-high, handheld camera movement occurs when El Hadji and Modu walk together on the street after the confiscation of El Hadji's business. El Hadji is moving ever more falteringly, leaning on Modu's arm simply to hold himself up. We have passed beyond the sleek, ironic combination of minaret and male posterior depth to a more indeterminate mode of pathos. Yet the sudden, strange, high-angle shot peering down towards the stool Modu is loyally carrying in his right hand is soon cut to a medium two-shot of El Hadji and Modu as the latter puts back on his black cap with its white strap – the opportunity for us to appreciate that Modu's clothing is, like that of the undesirables and Rama, never uniform, and can vary from a short-sleeved cream cotton jacket and matching trousers with either blue or orange T-shirt as here, to a more formal white cloth suit with white cap and shirt and tie, rendering Modu also a vehicle of variation and difference. Meanwhile, in between the two figures, standing tall and erect in the middle of the frame, is again the phallic minaret of the Grand Mosque.

No sooner have we had the chance to enjoy this barbed composition of verticality gone awry than a dry cut takes us to another flagrant handheld shot: a low-angle, close-up view of Gorgui's phallic staff in the centre of a frame of cloudy blue, gently revealed as a painted wall. It wobbles freely up and down before the camera pulls out, enough for us to realise that it is being carried forward by Gorgui in a lateral tracking shot. Used as a walking stick, and with its human-looking head lacking identifiable gender, the staff seems to be moving autonomously like an animated phallus. This combination of phallic and non-gendered elements remains troubling in its ambivalence, leading Green-Simms to claim that the phallic walking stick serves to replace the image of the phallic mosque.[66] Certainly, the sequence reveals that the undesirables – even the visually impaired Gorgui – can also figure within the film's phallic economy of visuality and verticality which otherwise they patently contest.

Although the full implications of Gorgui's penile staff will only be disclosed in the denouement, *Xala*'s original audience would already have a premonition due to a striking publicity poster. It presents a visual montage of power relations (class, gender, ethnic) where Gorgui, in the middle ground, is pictured frontally with his staff in his right fist pointed towards N'Goné, who is viewed from behind radiating out warm waves from the concealed front side of her body (only the middle third of her naked back and buttocks lying in the foreground is visible). It is as if Gorgui were rising erect out of her torso, while eclipsed in silhouette in the right background a diminutive, besuited El Hadji stumbles off with his attaché case. Our attention is drawn here to N'Goné's faceless, almost anonymous

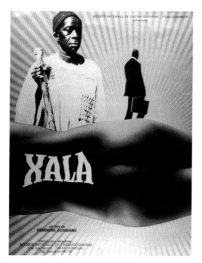

The original Senegalese publicity poster

voluptuousness, rather than to any line of sexual attraction.[67] We will soon discover in the narrative that El Hadji had originally stolen Gorgui's land – the means for Gorgui to ensure the continuity of his family in the countryside. Hence, the poster, where Gorgui's staff occupies with its anthropomorphic head the place of El Hadji's phallus, serves as a presentiment of his eventual act of retaliation which will entail stripping El Hadji of the last vestments of his identity.

6 From Evian to Sputum: Abjection as Redemption

The ugly face-off between El Hadji and Kebe in the Chamber is just the warm-up for *Xala*'s final act, for Sembene is preparing the viewer for an even more explosive clash between another set of doubles. In African oral storytelling a climactic encounter usually occurs between two different types of trickster figure.[68] The blind beggar Gorgui, who will shortly reveal himself as El Hadji's nemesis, projects the model of a more just society, thus carrying forward the Wolof tradition of trickster heroes like Leuk the Hare who perform benevolent deeds. In particular, Gorgui epitomises the traditional trickster's knavish art of improvisation and uncanny skill: he has been carefully biding his time for the opportunity to take his revenge and will exact it when, immediately following the bailiff's visit, he learns from Modu of El Hadji's belief that he has been afflicted again by the *xala*. This was doubtlessly reimposed by Sérigne Mada after El Hadji's failure to address him by name (in an instance of selective amnesia, he claimed not even to recognise the *marabout*), whereupon the latter, enraged by such dishonour and denial, sat down calmly on the pavement to reverse his earlier operation. Gorgui is now ready to take full advantage of the news. Indeed, Modu, who clearly knows more about Gorgui's status and capabilities than he cares to admit to his boss, positively invites him to do something, and Gorgui responds accordingly: 'I can fix it, I can cure it, I wish for nothing, I don't want his [El Hadji's] wealth. You know where I am.'

   Gorgui's claim to be able to set a curse and provide a cure at no monetary cost attests to the undesirables' latent potential: they can undo the work of the *marabout* and lift the *xala* because, as will now be divulged, they put the curse on El Hadji originally. If El Hadji is not actually the victim of a new curse, then Gorgui's claim that he gave him the *xala* constitutes a devious tactic. But if El Hadji is indeed impotent again, then waiting until he is brought to his knees is no less crafty. Whatever the case, rather than a direct expression of either traditional or technical fetishism, the curse places magic and power in a rational context and at the disposal of those who are disenfranchised and powerless. Sembene is clearly differentiating here between noble beggars, witch doctors and false, greedy *marabouts*, for the undesirables become now like satirists and thus the real medical men in *Xala*.[69]

The band of twenty or so undesirables are in the ascendant as they head towards Awa's villa in a comfortable, policed, residential area near the sea. In this reverse spin on their earlier journey back into the city, they gather irresistible momentum through a series of back- and side-tracking shots, propelled by the sheer weight of the musician's dubbed song with its message of moral invincibility: 'The lion is courageous. / The lion is honest. / The lion cannot be deprived of the object of his desire for lack of courage.'[70] Unlike the merely symbolic takeover of the Chamber with its idealising, heroic pretensions, *Xala*'s second home invasion is a grassroots mobilisation whereby the rejected members of society trespass into a private domestic space and open it up to civil society. This vital distinction is captured visually in the way the undesirables ascend the steps from the road to reach the villa: where before a low-angle shot recorded the elite ascending vertically to the Chambre de Commerce, here a more inclusive, horizontal wide frame brings together the undesirables and El Hadji and his family, who now confront each other for the first time and on a level footing. However, although the undesirables don't trash the house, it is not a pretty sight. The all-male band force their way into the family space and, as they help themselves to imported foods and soft drinks in the kitchen fridge, two of their number intimidate the maid, who yells in protest. Crucially, the camera stands behind the maid as she is menaced; hence, while not directly occupying her subjective point of view, the viewer experiences events from her perspective. Adesokan

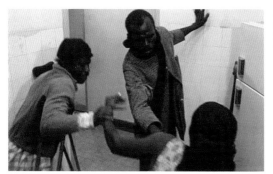

Awa's maid fending
off two undesirables
before being pushed
to the ground

notes that the impotent anger simmering during the earlier outdoor
coffee ceremony finds an outlet here in attacking an innocent
maid – a disturbing instance of the power of the powerless since it
also involves preying on their own kind, while also revealing the
contradictions of class consciousness.[71] Emerging sheepishly from
his bedroom in pyjamas, El Hadji asks rhetorically: 'What is this,
"robbery"?!', to which Gorgui retorts: 'No, vengeance!' Awa, herself
a victim of traditional patriarchy, tries to protect her husband by
ordering the invaders to leave, but they continue to raid the fridge,
the camera recording their plunder with documentary-like scrutiny.

Meanwhile, in the sitting room, the singer-musician is delicately
playing his *xalam* as if performing on stage, although his plaintive
song is again only heard and not witnessed 'live' by the viewer. The
mood is celebratory, for this is a beggars' feast arranged by and for
the undesirables in a satirical inversion of the wedding reception
from which they were excluded. Whereas before, consumed by the
daily graft of survival, they appeared dour and downtrodden, sullen
and suspicious, now they are convulsed and rejuvenated by laughter
and jesting (amplified on the soundtrack) and actively enjoying their
subversive company. The sense of a Bakhtinian carnival will shortly
be crystallised when one of the undesirables – the young car washer,
still wearing his paisley shirt plus brown waistcoat and carrying
Modu's blue bucket – removes the tiara from the wedding headdress

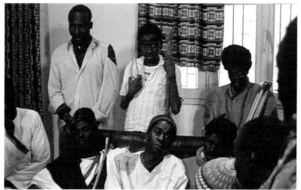

hanging on the mannequin and, to general amusement, places it on his head in mock solemnity. Western artefacts (comestibles, soft drinks, Christian wedding paraphernalia) are being brought together theatrically with symbolic African artefacts such as Gorgui's staff to form a potent new cultural hybrid that disrupts the customary codes of either Western or African fetishism.

When an armed policeman on patrol arrives at the front door, El Hadji, still in his pyjamas, reassures him that the undesirables are his guests, realising now that he cannot regain his power (sexual or economic) without the involvement of civil society which they represent. Rama is standing by her father's side and appears surprisingly demure compared to the feisty character of before. For the first time she condescends to speak French, confirming to the policeman that 'Papa has guests'. This shift in stance can perhaps be explained by the fact that Rama, like Sembene, does not completely reject the use of French in certain situations such as communicating with a representative of the state. She also surely knows what's in store for her father (nothing less than a moment of reckoning and last-ditch chance to redeem himself), so puts her family first. By simultaneously protecting the beggars who are allowed to stay, she is not only acting as before in the interests of civil society, but also defending the cause of her father, who depends on the undesirables' goodwill to regain his virility. The implication here is that the emancipation of the two groups – women and the poor – is fundamentally interrelated (Rama's brother Moctar remains, by contrast, all but irrelevant).

Once the policeman has duly left, the stage is set for the big reveal, initiated ironically by a second instance of misrecognition in the film. To Gorgui's simple question: 'Do you recognise me?', El Hadji responds in the negative. As with Sérigne Mada, this constitutes an act of repression: a conscious forgetting by El Hadji of his original means of ascension to the elite that necessitated Gorgui's descent into destitution.[72] The stakes of recognition could not be higher, for if El Hadji were to acknowledge the beggar, he would shatter his own

fantasy of being entitled to power. El Hadji's denial is the prompt
for Gorgui to begin his narrative, years in the making. We learn that
in a historic case of class theft, El Hadji dispossessed his illiterate
family, the Bèyes, of a plot of land that belonged to them by falsifying
the clan's names. He had his relative Gorgui imprisoned in order to
exploit their shared heritage for personal gain. Gorgui Bèye has thus
come to wreak vengeance on El Hadji for the crime of ousting him
and sending him to jail. Pointing to El Hadji he asserts virulently:
'What I am now is your fault.' El Hadji's betrayal of his kinsmen may
have taken place twenty years before, but tricksters are agents of
individual and collective memory.

In what Fredric Jameson has called 'a remarkable generic
transformation' in *Xala*'s narrative from satire to ritual and
prophecy,[73] the undesirables now assume another new guise – that
of a tribal jury. Gorgui formally declares: 'I arranged your *xala*,
the seer told you so' – a reference to Sérigne Mada rather than the
Président's *marabout*. He then gestures with his upturned finger
towards his young assistant behind him holding his staff, as if
acknowledging the power of vision as both the physical act of seeing
and the interpretive act of clairvoyance. 'You [El Hadji] ate all my
father's wealth, how could you get away with it?,' Gorgui snarls.
The peasant emissary also intervenes, claiming that El Hadji, having
lost all dignity and honour, has only his manhood left to restore.
The undesirables guffaw loudly. When one of their band warns the
police are nearby and that they should leave, Gorgui counteracts
with: 'We are his [El Hadji's] guests, and he wants to become a man
again!' Hilarity. The filmic narrative, we now realise, had always
been leading to this moment: El Hadji's *xala* was simply a pretext
for the main event of the excluded finally setting the terms of their
own inclusion within society and their accession to social status. It's a
return of the repressed as the socially suppressed, who now effectively
attain the position of political dissidents.

But El Hadji's ritual trial to regain virility – and Gorgui's act
of vengeance in the name of justice – will demand more than simply

words of derision. He is forced to strip naked (the camera limits itself to his upper torso) and is grotesquely crowned with the wedding tiara (a white-orange flower-like wreath with Christian resonances of the crown of thorns placed on the head of Jesus during the crucifixion) as a cruel reminder of the virginity of the woman he was unable to deflower. This pageant of humiliation and sacrifice is conducted like a fake wedding – an ironic inversion not only of the wedding night and El Hadji's abortive display of potency, but also of the morning after when his floundering masculinity was verbally shredded by three women. The tiara is being transformed before our eyes from a symbol of neocolonial fetishism into an agent of mystical purification (an object is never just an object in *Xala*). If one recalls that the tiara was returned by the trans figure, such feminising of El Hadji might also suggest a link back to the Western classical tradition of the blind Tiresias, a prophet of Apollo in Thebes famous for clairvoyancy and whose transgendered identity accorded him power. Certainly, while underlining the dominance of the blind Gorgui, this transfigurative ritual raises again the question of the relation between masculinity and race in the postcolony, for if the *xala* is categorically lifted and the cycle of El Hadji's passivity and symbolic (White) 'feminisation' reversed, what type of Black man will be reborn?

The laughter suddenly fades when Gorgui stands up with his phallic staff in his right hand and the camera slowly pulls back to a medium long shot of El Hadji, photographed from behind, stepping up onto a chair and taking off his shirt, surrounded on all sides by the undesirables. It is a purposely odd arrangement of sound and camera, and the inclusion of the rest of the family as observers behind the camera establishes an uneasy spatial relation for the viewer. Awa threatens to call security (after all, the sputum of some of the undesirables may carry disease), but to no avail – what must be will be. Now begins the final phase of this unprecedented ceremony when El Hadji, at tipping point, submits to the undesirables in an act of voluntary abjection. They draw gobs of phlegm from the depths of

their throats and shoot them like bullets at El Hadji's face and body.
As Harrow writes, this is El Hadji's final ordeal as a failed trickster:
a descent into the ordure of the abject, the liminal space occupied out
of necessity by the trickster.[74]

Yet while this devastating scene of disgust could not be more
real and visceral, Sembene insists, as in the pre-credits sequence, on a
bifurcation of sound and image. Although transported to a close-up
of El Hadji's abjectified, naked chest and back as the slime slowly
oozes down his skin, we are denied the audiovisual satisfaction
of seeing spit being ejected and landing on its target. Instead, the

A close-up of El Hadji's bespattered back as the camera circles round

sounds of spitting are heightened by the muteness of other images, for example, Moctar's aghast face. A further denaturalising formal tension is created by the movement of the camera, which, as El Hadji moves clockwise, proceeds in an anti-clockwise direction. It first pans around the figure of El Hadji, the spittle covering his shoulders and chest, then opens up to a medium shot of his son and daughter transfixed, before lingering on an intimate image of Awa sobbing at the sight of her husband's degradation. Typically, this is not a tidy manoeuvre: the camera does not record a full 360-degree circle, as if highlighting the sordid messiness of the ritual which is ultimately left more to our imagination through the literally gut-wrenching sounds that feel all the more deafening and disgusting for taking place off-screen. When we do behold El Hadji's back scored with thick, white globules (a darkly ironic echo of the hyper-white items of the wedding), it has far more granulated spit on it than has logically been ejected.

Let us savour the delicious irony here: not only is El Hadji's morally abject and emasculated body being (potentially) restored again to manhood through its very abasement, but this is happening by the grace of those abjected from neocolonial society and their foul, bodily excretions. Put differently, a blatantly repulsive display of human waste – a spectacular revenge of the 'dirt' in *Xala* – is playing out organically as the transformation of human matter, as if, in an ultimate formal paradox, one can cure one form of abjection by another. Saliva in modest quantities is sometimes used in African religious ceremonies, but Sembene freely acknowledged that the spitting ritual does not actually exist in Senegalese society (although he emphasised that when something disgusts the Senegalese, they draw spit from the depths of their throat and throw it sideways).[75] How, therefore, to apprehend it? For Harrow, the ritual functions as an expiatory ceremony of forgiveness, for in tales of the *marabout* 'saliva is the concrete means by which the parole and baraka of the holy man is to be transferred to the petitioner'.[76] For Pfaff, the beggars' ejaculatory spitting has a spiritual, moral and physical regenerative function – a rite of passage from one state of being to another.[77] John Mbiti, meanwhile, confirms that many sexual offences are 'followed by a ritual cleansing whether or not the offenders are physically punished, otherwise misfortunes may ensue'.[78]

But the exorcism of collective spitting is also an emphatic denouncement of both El Hadji and the elite. If, as Gabriel notes, El Hadji becomes literally the 'incarnation' of all members of the class or group that spit on him and reintegrate him into folk society after his moral death, the vomiting of bile constitutes also a symbolic social act: the common people's expression of anger against the bourgeoisie.[79] Landy argues further that the punishment of spitting as cure is elevated to an act of virtual revolution, encouraged by the musician's non-diegetic song with its appeal to revolt.[80] Indeed, the previously voiceless, excluded masses acquire a new revolutionary language, for to spit is to speak back – an elemental form of *prise de parole* (or speaking out politically to be heard), taken to the point where the human voice and orality break down into the materiality of pure sound. That said, on a strictly linguistic level, the momentous act of spitting may also carry an implicit and paradoxical warning: stray too far from the authentic gut of African languages and culture by importing cultural values and you risk turning indigenous language into discord, and with it the male body into an object of disgust.

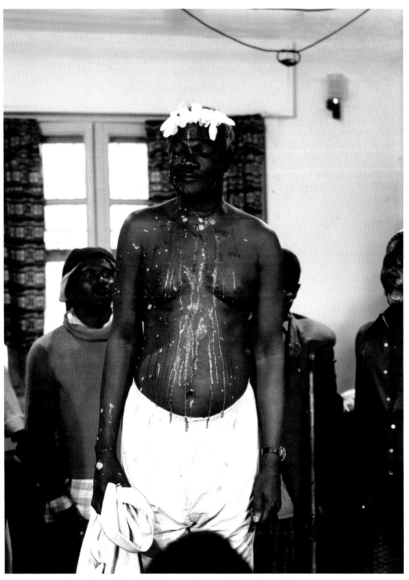

A medium shot of El Hadji's face and torso during the spitting ceremony

As we try to absorb how sticky, semen-like globules of sputum can become alchemically an affirmative political metaphor and help cure the body politic, the ceremony is abruptly cut short and suspended by a freeze frame, the French title '*fin*' ('The end') arriving two seconds later in blood red, echoing the film's opening crimson credits. A definitive split between sound and image has thus been engineered, so that the final experience of *Xala* is one of formal differentiation and fissure. '*Fin*' rests in the middle of the frame with El Hadji at an angle on the right looking off-screen. Time, El Hadji and his potential redemption are now visually suspended, although on the soundtrack the spitting continues apace. The already exaggerated sounds of expectoration appear further magnified by the absence of any visual movement: we are left staring as if into the void of blinding disgust. Nine seconds later, the printed image disappears completely, superseded by a black screen without any closing credits, making altogether forty-five seconds of auditory spitting.

In purely narrative terms, *Xala* is thus brought to a halt before providing any conclusive evidence that the spitting has had a curative or redemptive effect (i.e. El Hadji's rehabilitation), with the result that the various occult and psychological explanations for El Hadji's affliction (a revenge curse, psychosomatic illness) all still remain valid. The lack both of narrative closure and of a clean resolution to the film's restless, audiovisual contagion leaves us literally in the dirty mess of uncertainty, provoking, as intended, countless interpretations and speculations. For Green-Simms, the freeze-frame ending that both freezes time and moves the soundtrack forward, and where El Hadji's paused naked body being spat on is exposed literally without a carapace, reinforces the idea of a perpetually stalling, stuttering and insurmountable postcolonial present.[81] For Landy, by extending into a darkened place as if reverting to the recesses of the mind (to memory, or maybe unconsciousness), *Xala* makes the audience privy to the futility of replacing one group of autocratic men with another without radically changing the economic and social structures in Senegal.[82] For Mulvey, on the other hand, the ending 'signals a lifting of amnesia and acceptance of history […] the freeze frame resur-erects [*sic*] a man, whole through community, stripped of the trappings of colonialism and fetishised individualism.'[83] This affirmative reading accords with Harrow's idea that the cleansing ritual marks the restoration of community, with El Hadji serving as a form of sacrifice, for by the end he is 'no longer the prick, object of the camera's scorn, but now the figure of passage, the trickster who has made himself into the sign of the limen, the wooden phallus'.[84] Other, more non-committal interpretations reflect the fundamentally ambivalent nature of the ceremony. For Matthew Brown, for instance, it is a calculated structural inversion – an act meant to reclaim the system by which the elite has been allowed to hijack the nation, but without destroying the foundations of the structure itself. The film's cautionary message, Brown argues, is that the people need to 'break in' and 'spew' their lack of representation over all the body politic, for at the very least civil society must achieve incorporation on its own terms and convince the state of this. The bourgeoisie is thus left with a choice: either to alienate civil society again, or work to introduce revolutionary reforms.[85]

 Yet in a film as critically self-aware and metacinematic as *Xala*, there is another avenue of critique that must be considered in any final reading – one that returns us literally to Sembene's own place within Senegalese and African cinema more generally. I am not simply referring to the poster visible in Moctar's room announcing the screening of *La Noire de …* (this after an earlier glimpse of a poster for *Mandabi* in Rama's room), or to the blood-like '*fin*' that evokes the final intertitle '*fin de cinéma*' of Godard's *Week-end* – we are, after all, well used to *Xala*'s self-referential techniques involving Second Cinema. More fundamentally, Awa's home is actually Sembene's own house in the Dakar suburb of Yoff, which he built himself and called 'Galle Ceddo' (Rebel House). As Adesokan argues, the fact that Sembene's role as a politically engaged film-maker is closely scripted into the final sequence foregrounds his position as a committed artist-activist rooted in aesthetic populism – that is, he is making films that speak to the yearnings of a broad population in Senegal and Africa as a whole. While Sembene liked to describe himself as a modern *griot* storyteller working in the popular narrative form of cinema, Adesokan rightly considers him more a trickster-god of storytelling who acted like a cunning fox, collaborating with the neocolonial funding institutions of Senegalese cinema to produce an anti-neocolonialist film intent on attacking them.[86]

However, the filmic self-exposure and self-consciousness at the end of *Xala* may also be part of Sembene's political project to, as Landy puts it, use film language self-consciously to defetishise itself.[87] For Sembene's mode of self-presentation not only sustains a commentary on his own practice (and the fact that cinema, wherever it may take place, is by its nature rarely a free, 'traditional', communal gathering[88]), but also works to make that practice resistant to the fetishising of yet another commodity, namely *Xala* as a commercial product within the global network of entertainment. The defiantly open and incomplete ending – a stirring call to imagine the politically impossible – could thus also be viewed as a way for Sembene to pre-empt the risks of self-fetishisation and of African cinema as its own fetish. If, as Fardon suggests of the undesirables, it is only by 'admitting the abjected in all their horror to the sanctum of the family' that a society can begin to find the means of making peace with itself,[89] then the same may be said of Sembene: that it is only by fully recognising and representing within his own private space the abjection of the prohibitively expensive Western form and system of commercial cinema (obscenely wasteful if placed within the general context of poverty and suffering in Africa) that he might ever be able to cure the curse of African cinema (a product so far underwritten by and for the elite) by making it progressive, inclusive and open to the people he wishes to reach. The case of *Xala*, poised always between consumer entertainment and political commitment, would seem to suggest that this is potentially possible (another instance of the inherent temporariness of the *xala*) on account of its insistence on difficulty and complication, ambivalence and paradox – the very hallmarks of Third Cinema indigestibility. Seen from this perspective, the unresolved tensions, frictions and imperfections of *Xala* appear the very conditions of a radical, postcolonial, film practice.

Epilogue: The Legacy of *Xala*

With its daring combination of critique, comedy and sheer aesthetic
verve and power, *Xala* is a visionary work – a luminous, enthralling,
tempestuous, and at times incendiary, mix of styles, themes and
tonalities. It vividly captured the period of social, cultural and
political upheaval in 1970s Senegal, while also showing how the
ravages of neocolonialism are directly inscribed on the human body.
Yet *Xala*'s open defiance and provocative unruliness also affected
its release. Since it was part-funded by the SNC (an arrangement
Sembene later described as a fiasco), the government imposed
ten cuts: the Marianne bust and the attaché cases being opened
in the pre-credits sequence; El Hadji's declaration to members of
the Chamber that they have the police and army in their pockets;
Gorgui's judgment that prisoners are happier than peasants,
fishermen or workers; the closing call to revolt; and all the scenes
featuring the White chief of police who looked uncannily like
Senghor's Minister of the Interior, Jean Collin – a White Frenchman,
naturalised Senegalese. Sembene complied by reshooting two scenes
and altering the appearance of the commissioner, although he also
resisted this crude censorship by distributing flyers detailing the
scenes that had been cut. It remained for him a bitter irony that a
film intended primarily for the Senegalese could only be viewed in
its entirety abroad. However, this did not prevent *Xala* from being
the popular critical and commercial success Sembene had coveted.
It came second in 1975 at the Senegalese box office after (typically)
a Bruce Lee kung fu action film. Murphy notes that the 'socialist
fetishism' in *Xala*, particularly in the final sequence where the viewer
is left to ponder the meaning of political and supernatural acts,
proved especially successful with Senegalese audiences.[90] Anecdotally,
Mercedes cars became suspect for three months in Dakar – no one

wished to be seen driving such models for fear they might be publicly assailed like El Hadji with the charge of thief, opportunist and victim of the *xala*. As was Sembene's custom, he toured the country to project and personally introduce *Xala* to local audiences. The film quickly became – and would remain – Sembene's greatest commercial success in Africa.

The decision to distribute *Xala* internationally in 1975 was taken by the French company Union Générale Cinématographique (UGC) (the Senegalese government's partner created in 1971) and the new distribution company, SIDEC. The film was released commercially in France and the US and shown at the Moscow, Rotterdam, Locarno, New York and Cannes film festivals. It won the Special Prize at the Karlovy Vary Festival in Czechoslovakia and the Silver Medal at the Figueira da Foz International Film Festival in Portugal. Critical responses were for the most part highly enthusiastic. John Ngara wrote in *Africa* that while the film's 'structure and substance give it an unmistakable Africanness [...] *Xala* is capable of reaching virtually anyone because its message is simple, straightforward and succinct'.[91] Udayan Gupta in the *N.Y. Amsterdam News* considered *Xala* a 'magnificent critique of the neo-colonial structures that have sprouted from the ruins of colonialism'.[92] Kathleen McCaffrey in *Africa Report* hailed *Xala* as both a satire of the Black bourgeoisie and a condemnation of polygamy.[93] Seeking to place the film in a Western framework, Alain Masson wrote in *Positif* that its fierce humour summoned up Aristophanes and that the final spitting scene appeared a reworking of Luis Buñuel's *Viridiana* (1961).[94] There was, however, the odd dissenting voice, notably the Tunisian critic and future film-maker Férid Boughedir, who, in *Jeune Afrique*, claimed *Xala* was Sembene's least convincing film owing to its excessive use of caricature, dualistic over-schematisation (rich vs poor, good vs evil) and its 'technically botched' ending.[95] Similarly, Tom Dowling in the *Washington Star*, while celebrating *Xala*'s ferocious critique (the 'unexpected bite in an African filmmaker bitterly tearing into his own country's roots'), regretted the film's 'technical difficulties'.[96] This, of course, deliberately disregarded the aims of Third Cinema. Yet, as the Tunisian film critic Noureddine Ghali pointed out in *Cinéma 76*, the international context of *Xala* was not merely America nor France. Citing the film's impact on audiences at the 1976 Bombay Film Festival, Ghali wrote that '*Xala* reflects, like a mirror, a faithful image not only of an African country, but also of the Third World.'[97] In *Newsweek* Jack Kroll went further, declaring that on the basis of *Xala* Sembene was one of the most remarkable contemporary world artists.[98]

Xala cemented Sembene's status as a politically engaged pan-African film-maker while also positioning him as a new kind of African auteur – the pioneer of a radical African modernism with an unflinching 'metacolonial' vision.[99] Prior to its release Sembene told Tahar Cheriaa that African film-makers had a mission to prepare for revolution and incite revolt:

That's what he [the true artist] is needed for, that's how he can achieve glory, but that's also his shortcoming. Others will always make revolutions, just as he will always set the stage for it through clarifying, analyzing, revealing, and calling out things. He implants in the minds of others the clear conviction that *revolution is necessary and feasible* (original emphasis).[100]

As Sembene also explained to Ghali, collective struggle against injustice was the only way to avert catastrophe and violence: 'the powers-that-be […], if we do not get rid of them, will tomorrow be trees which are going to overrun the place and have to be cut down'.[101] Pushing always for genuine structural change and political freedom, Sembene's censure of Senghor persisted, and he remained both prolific and politically active until his death in 2007. In 1976, he began work on a book entitled *Le Dernier de l'empire* (*The Last of the Empire*), published in 1981, that dealt with a set of characters similar to those in *Xala* caught up in a *coup d'état* against the president of an African country who has outstayed his democratic welcome and mysteriously disappeared. In fact, Senghor left office peacefully in 1980, but not before banning Sembene's 1977 film *Ceddo*, supposedly because the title was apparently misspelt but really out of fear that the film might offend the large Muslim electorate on which he relied for support.

The influence of *Xala* on the course of African cinema has been extensive and far-reaching. It soon became, almost despite itself, a kind of fetish within African film studies. During the mid-1980s it was the subject of an intense dispute in the journal *Screen* between self-styled 'form and content' critics like Gabriel and Roy Armes, and 'cine-semioticians' (or cine-Structuralists) such as Ella Shohat and Robert Stam. They disagreed about which theoretical mode was most appropriate for the analysis of African films. However, all recognised *Xala* as a defining work of both African cinema and Third Cinema, and it later served as the cornerstone of the sequence on African cinema in Mark Cousins's 2011 television documentary, *The Story of Film: An Odyssey*. Following the release of the well-received documentary *Sembene!* (2015), directed by Jason Silverman and Sembene's longstanding mentee Samba Gadjigo,[102] there is renewed global interest in Sembene's work, even though his films have yet to achieve their full intended audience in Africa owing to the perpetual difficulties of censorship, distribution and exhibition.

For the millennial generation of African film-makers attempting to address the new realities of Africa, *Xala*'s generative metaphors and replotting of urban space have provided a dazzling springboard for posing fresh and uncomfortable questions about the ongoing processes of neocolonialism, geopolitical poverty, the role of women and social justice. Indeed, with its highly prescient themes of urban displacement, social cleansing and gentrification, and its depiction of a sprawling, urban cine-scape outstripping the clear spatial boundaries previously mapped in Senegalese cinema, *Xala* offers a still crucially relevant and timely vision of the emerging Afropolis under the multiple stresses of rapid population growth, insufficient

The communal everyday intruding into the trial as it is being filmed in *Bamako* (2006)

infrastructure and corrupt governance. It has inspired a number of films set in Dakar such as *Tey/Today* (2013) by the French-Senegalese director Alain Gomis, and *Atlantique/Atlantics* (2019) by another French-Senegalese film-maker, Mati Diop. The latter features a scene directly recalling *Xala*'s final spitting ritual: the moment when the ghost women stand in feminist solidarity in a living room demanding retribution for wrongs done, notably the undelivered cheques that force young men to risk their lives attempting to migrate across the ocean to Europe.

Xala's lasting legacy as a model of engaged, postcolonial art cinema informs the work of the contemporary Mauritanian director Abderrahmane Sissako, who, by common consent, has assumed with Sembene's passing the mantle of Africa's most influential and politically significant film-maker. Although very different in register, Sissako's 2006 film *Bamako*, which attempts to combat the structures of neoliberalism and neocolonial economic policies implemented across Africa since the mid-1980s by putting on trial the IMF and World Bank, is a similarly hybrid, multi-form and multi-genre work incorporating documentary and fictional elements. It cultivates an open, non-hierarchising frame welcoming the mutual intrusion of the voices and lives of local people attempting to resist the daily threats to civic society and shared notions of community.[103] Like *Xala*, *Bamako* lays bare both the governing elite (now globalised) and the capitalist system of cinema itself, confronting some of the key underlying questions of the medium addressed by Sembene, most urgently whether film, despite its commercial constraints, possesses the potential to help advance social change by aesthetic means and pave the way for transformation in postcolonial African cultures. Such questions remain still to be fully answered, yet by raising them so acutely and inventively with its exhilarating story of dissent, solidarity and collective action, *Xala* continues to burn bright in African and World Cinema as a beacon of political hope.

Notes

1 See Josef Gugler and Oumar Chérif Diop, 'Ousmane Sembène's *Xala*: The Novel, the Film, and Their Audiences', in Ernest Cole and Oumar Chérif Diop (eds), *Ousmane Sembène: Writer, Filmmaker, and Revolutionary Artist* (Trenton, NJ: Africa World Press, 2016), pp. 283–96 (291n5).
2 'Doomireew' means 'the country's child' in Wolof.
3 Published by Présence Africaine (Paris).
4 See Paulin Soumanou Vieyra, *Sembène Ousmane, cinéaste: première période 1962–1971* (Paris: Présence Africaine, 2012 [1972]). *Xala* also credits the participation of the co-director of Vieyra's pioneering short *Afrique sur Seine* (1955), Mamadou Sarr, who plays one of the unnamed members of the Chamber.
5 Ousmane Sembene, *L'Harmattan* (Paris: Présence Africaine, 1980 [1964]), p. 9.
6 Rachel Diang'a, 'Trans-formal Aesthetics and Cultural Impact on Ousmane Sembène's *Xala*', in Lifongo Vetinde and Amadou T. Fofana (eds), *Ousmane Sembène and the Politics of Culture* (Lanham, MD: Lexington Books, 2014). Kindle version. Location 3340.
7 Mauritanians dominated the retail grocery trade in Senegal until riots against them in 1989. El Hadji's eleventh-hour proposal to the bank to establish retail outlets in a 'native area' in order to remain in business constitutes a nationalist project since he is effectively playing the national card.
8 See Nwachukwu Frank Ukadike, *Black African Cinema* (Berkeley: University of California Press, 1994), pp. 178–9.

9 Even today, while around 80 per cent of Senegalese speak Wolof (one of Senegal's national languages) as their first or second language, less than 30 per cent are fluent in French, which remains the official language. For a study of Senghor's cultural policies, see Joshua I. Cohen, 'African Socialist Cultural Policy: Senegal Under Senghor', *African Arts* 54, no. 3 (2021), pp. 28–37.
10 Cited in Noureddine Ghali, 'Interview with Ousmane Sembène' [1976], in Annett Busch and Max Annas (eds), *Ousmane Sembène: Interviews*, trans. John D. H. Downing (Jackson: University Press of Mississippi, 2008), pp. 72–81 (79).
11 See Gugler and Diop, 'Ousmane Sembène's *Xala*', pp. 288–9.
12 Cited in David Murphy, 'The Indiscreet Charm of the African Bourgeoisie?: Consumerism, Fetishism and Socialism in *Xala*', in *Sembene: Imagining Alternatives in Film and Fiction*, trans. David Murphy (Oxford: James Currey, 2000), pp. 98–123 (115).
13 Ibid., p. 110.
14 Teshome H. Gabriel, '*Xala*: A Cinema of Wax and Gold', *Jump Cut* 27 (July 1982), pp. 31–3. Available at: <https://www.ejumpcut.org/archive/onlineessays/JC27folder/XalaGabriel.html> (accessed 2 October 2022).
15 Marcia Landy, 'Political Allegory and "Engaged Cinema": Sembene's *Xala*' [1984], in Ernest Cole and Oumar Chérif Diop (eds), *Ousmane Sembène: Writer, Filmmaker, and Revolutionary Artist* (Trenton, NJ: Africa World Press, 2016), pp. 177–92 (186).
16 See Octavio Getino and Fernando Solanas, 'Toward a Third

Cinema', *Tricontinental* 14 (1969), pp. 107–32. Available at: <https://ufsinfronteradotcom.files.wordpress.com/2011/05/tercer-cine-getino-solanas-19691.pdf> (accessed 11 October 2022).

17 David Murphy, 'The Cinematic Representation of Post-Independence Africa: Culture, Capitalism and Neo-Colonialism in *Xala* and *Touki-Bouki*', *ASCALF Bulletin* 20 (2000), pp. 21–37 (25).

18 Rocha's 1965 manifesto 'The Aesthetics of Hunger' is available at: <https://www.amherst.edu/media/view/38122/original/ROCHA_Aesth_Hunger.pdf> (accessed 3 November 2022).

19 Karen Redrobe Beckman, *Crash: Cinema and the Politics of Speed and Stasis* (Durham, NC: Duke University Press, 2010), pp. 205–34.

20 In reality, this was a villa in Dakar's consular area owned by an American director of foreign aid.

21 Lucy Fischer, '*Xala*: A Study in Black Humor', *Millennium Film Journal* 7–9 (1980–1), pp. 165–72 (167).

22 Françoise Pfaff points out that women beggars are absent from this dispossessed brotherhood for reasons both of symbolic continuity (the curse of male impotency is imposed and potentially removed by the same leader of the undesirables) and verisimilitude (female beggars are mostly seen on the streets of downtown Dakar with young children). See Françoise Pfaff, 'Three Faces of Africa: Women in *Xala*', *Jump Cut* 27 (July 1982), pp. 27–31. Available at: <https://www.ejumpcut.org/archive/onlineessays/JC27folder/XalaPfaff.html> (accessed 25 September 2022).

23 Landy, 'Political Allegory and "Engaged Cinema"', p. 188.

24 Gabriel, '*Xala*: A Cinema of Wax and Gold'.

25 Lindsey B. Green-Simms, *Postcolonial Automobility: Car Culture in West Africa* (Minneapolis: University of Minnesota Press, 2017), pp. 89–105 (98).

26 Laura Mulvey, '*Xala*, Ousmane Sembene (1974): The Carapace That Failed', in Ernest Cole and Oumar Chérif Diop (eds), *Ousmane Sembène: Writer, Filmmaker, and Revolutionary Artist* (Trenton, NJ: Africa World Press, 2016), pp. 407–26 (420).

27 See Richard Fardon and Sènga la Rouge, *Learning from the Curse: Sembene's* Xala (London: C. Hurst & Co., 2017), p. 73.

28 Akin Adesokan, *Postcolonial Artists and Global Aesthetics* (Bloomington: University of Indiana Press, 2011), p. 75.

29 In an overwhelmingly Muslim country like Senegal, most people carry charms for personal protection from malevolent forces and believe in the capacity of others to attack them using such powers. See Fardon and La Rouge, *Learning from the Curse*, p. 75.

30 Landy, 'Political Allegory and "Engaged Cinema"', p. 185.

31 Fardon and La Rouge, *Learning from the Curse*, p. 84.

32 Cited in Murphy, 'The Indiscreet Charm of the African Bourgeoisie?', p. 108.

33 Ibid., p. 77.

34 This knowingly 'deficient' sequence has led Mowitt to argue that the failed

act of marital copulation is mimed and
repeated in the semiotics of the film,
which employs two different syntaxes
corresponding to French and Wolof.
The mirror vs photograph parallel is
a case in point, since the stasis of the
photograph, at once immobile and
atemporal, is an instance of nominal
syntax, a pattern more associated with
Wolof. Mowitt reveals how, through
the false match-on-action shot,
the sequence skips the attempted
consummation and literally suspends
the act of copulation, which is here
both sexual and a 'language shot'.
See John Mowitt, *Re-takes: Postcoloniality
and Foreign Film Languages* (Minneapolis:
Minnesota University Press, 2005),
pp. 104, 115–16.
35 Ibid., p. 110.
36 Green-Simms, *Postcolonial
Automobility*, p. 95.
37 Ibid., p. 89.
38 Tahar Cheriaa, 'Issues in African
Film: The Artist and the Revolution:
"Interview with Ousmane Sembene
[1974]"', trans. Moustapha Diop,
Framework 61, no. 2 (2020), pp. 12–22
(12–13).
39 Pfaff, 'Three Faces of Africa: Women
in *Xala*'.
40 Ibid.
41 See John S. Mbiti, *African Religions and
Philosophy* (New York: Doubleday, 1969),
p. 186.
42 Cited in Pfaff, 'Three Faces of Africa:
Women in *Xala*'.
43 Pfaff, 'Three Faces of Africa: Women
in *Xala*'.
44 Adesokan, *Postcolonial Artists and
Global Aesthetics*, p. 66.

45 Kenneth W. Harrow, 'Sembene
Ousmane's *Xala*: The Use of Film and
Novel as Revolutionary Weapon',
in Ernest Cole and Oumar Chérif
Diop (eds), *Ousmane Sembène: Writer,
Filmmaker, and Revolutionary Artist*
(Trenton, NJ: Africa World Press, 2016),
pp. 361–70 (362).
46 Ibid., p. 364.
47 Green-Simms, *Postcolonial
Automobility*, p. 96.
48 Ibid., pp. 100–2.
49 Fardon and La Rouge, *Learning from
the Curse*, p. 41.
50 Sheila Petty, 'Towards a Changing
Africa: Women's Roles in the Films
of Ousmane Sembene', in Sheila
Petty (ed.), *A Call to Action: The Films
of Ousmane Sembene* (Westport, CT:
Greenwood Press, 1996), pp. 67–86 (71).
51 The unique colour combination
differs from the conventional pan-
African colours of red, black and green.
52 Mowitt, *Re-takes*, p. 104.
53 Adesokan, *Postcolonial Artists and
Global Aesthetics*, pp. 70–1.
54 Fardon and La Rouge, *Learning from
the Curse*, p. 87.
55 Aaron Mushengyezi, 'Reimaging
Gender and African Tradition? Ousmane
Sembene's *Xala* Revisited', in Ernest
Cole and Oumar Chérif Diop (eds),
*Ousmane Sembène: Writer, Filmmaker, and
Revolutionary Artist* (Trenton, NJ: Africa
World Press, 2016), pp. 317–32.
56 Adesokan, *Postcolonial Artists and
Global Aesthetics*, p. 62.
57 Kenneth W. Harrow, 'Sembène's *Xala*,
the Fetish, and the Failed Trickster',
in *Postcolonial African Cinema: From
Political Engagement to Postmodernism*

(Bloomington: Indiana University Press, 2007), pp. 44–65 (54).

58 The bags of rice are labelled SIPA (Société Importation de Produits Alimentaires), a food-supplier that still operates in Senegal.

59 Harrow, 'Sembène's *Xala*, the Fetish, and the Failed Trickster', p. 55.

60 Ibid., p. 56.

61 Fardon and La Rouge, *Learning from the Curse*, p. 118.

62 We note that after being issued on VHS video, *Xala* was cropped to 1.37:1 ratio. It meant that its wide-frame, horizontal effects are not always guaranteed and visual material on the left and right of the screen is occasionally missing. Another scene where this occurs is the family quarrel at Awa's house.

63 Teshome H. Gabriel, 'Towards a Critical Theory of Third World Films', *Critical Interventions* 5, no. 1 (2011), pp. 187–203 (198).

64 See Mulvey, '*Xala*, Ousmane Sembene (1974)', p. 419.

65 Ibid., p. 417.

66 Green-Simms, *Postcolonial Automobility*, p. 102.

67 See Fardon and La Rouge, *Learning from the Curse*, p. 86.

68 See Thomas J. Lynn, 'Politics, Plunder, and Postcolonial Tricksters: Ousmane Sembène's *Xala*', in Ernest Cole and Oumar Chérif Diop (eds), *Ousmane Sembène: Writer, Filmmaker, and Revolutionary Artist* (Trenton, NJ: Africa World Press, 2016), pp. 371–90 (377–81).

69 See Landy, 'Political Allegory and "Engaged Cinema"', p. 189. Landy reminds us that satire originated historically in magical and healing practices.

70 Cited in Gugler and Diop, 'Ousmane Sembène's *Xala*', p. 289.

71 Adesokan, *Postcolonial Artists and Global Aesthetics*, pp. 70–1.

72 See Mulvey, '*Xala*, Ousmane Sembene (1974)', p. 420.

73 Fredric Jameson, 'Third-World Literature in the Era of Multinational Capitalism', *Social Text* 13 (1986), pp. 65–88 (84).

74 Harrow, 'Sembène's *Xala*, the Fetish, and the Failed Trickster', p. 48.

75 Cited in Mushengyezi, 'Reimaging Gender and African Tradition?', p. 329.

76 Harrow, 'Sembène's *Xala*, the Fetish, and the Failed Trickster', p. 61.

77 Pfaff, 'Three Faces of Africa: Women in *Xala*'.

78 Mbiti, *African Religions and Philosophy*, p. 193.

79 Gabriel, '*Xala*: A Cinema of Wax and Gold'.

80 Landy, 'Political Allegory and "Engaged Cinema"', p. 183.

81 Green-Simms, *Postcolonial Automobility*, p. 108.

82 Landy, 'Political Allegory and "Engaged Cinema"', pp. 190–1.

83 Mulvey, '*Xala*, Ousmane Sembene (1974)', p. 425.

84 Harrow, 'Sembène's *Xala*, the Fetish, and the Failed Trickster', p. 63.

85 Matthew H. Brown, 'Bringing the Rain Indoors: Rereading the National Allegory in Ousmane Sembène's *Xala*', in Lifongo Vetinde and Amadou T. Fofana (eds), *Ousmane Sembène and the Politics of Culture* (Lanham, MD: Lexington Books, 2014). Kindle version.

86 Adesokan, *Postcolonial Artists and Global Aesthetics*, p. 79.

87 Landy, 'Political Allegory and "Engaged Cinema"', pp. 187–8.

88 See Murphy, 'The Cinematic Representation of Post-Independence Africa', p. 23.

89 Fardon and La Rouge, *Learning from the Curse*, p. 122.

90 Murphy, 'The Indiscreet Charm of the African Bourgeoisie?', p. 123.

91 John Ngara, '*Xala* – An Allegory on Celluloid', *Africa* 64 (December 1976), p. 51.

92 Udayan Gupta, 'The Watchful Eye of Ousmane Sembene', *N.Y. Amsterdam News*, 11 February 1978, p. B12.

93 Kathleen McCaffrey, 'African Women on the Screen', *Africa Report* 26, no. 2 (March–April 1981), pp. 56–8 (57).

94 Alain Masson, 'Mascarade à Dakar', *Positif* 182 (June 1976), pp. 54–6 (56).

95 Férid Boughedir, 'Une Parabole des privilégiés', *Jeune Afrique* 795, 2 April 1976, pp. 56–8 (57).

96 Tom Dowling, 'Two New Movies: The Impotence of a Groom and His Country', *Washington Star*, 28 September 1977, pp. B1, B4.

97 Noureddine Ghali, '*Xala*, histoire symbolique d'une déchéance', *Cinéma 76*, no. 208 (April 1976), p. 95.

98 Jack Kroll, 'The World on Film', *Newsweek*, 13 October 1975, pp. 103–4 (103).

99 This is Sembene's own term, cited by John Mowitt in a post-screening Q&A on *Xala* at Walker Art Center, Minneapolis, on 13 November 2010. Available at: <https:www.youtube.com/watch?v=COimAotPgGo> (accessed 5 February 2023).

100 Cheriaa, 'Issues in African Film: The Artist and the Revolution', p. 15.

101 Ghali, 'Interview with Ousmane Sembène', p. 79.

102 See also Samba Gadjigo's biography, *Ousmane Sembene: The Making of a Militant Artist* (Bloomington: University of Indiana Press, 2010), which covers mainly Sembene's career as a writer. An earlier Senegalese film on Sembene was *Sembène: The Making of African Cinema* (1994), directed by Ngugi Wa Thiong'o and the African film scholar Manthia Diawara, whose book *African Film: New Forms of Aesthetics and Politics* (Munich: Prestel, 2010) insists on the vital, ongoing legacy of Sembene.

103 For a critical analysis of *Bamako*, see James S. Williams, *Ethics and Aesthetics in Contemporary African Cinema: The Politics of Beauty* (London: Bloomsbury, 2019), pp. 61–81.

Credits

Xala
Senegal
1974

Directed by
Ousmane Sembene
Screenplay
Ousmane Sembene
Based on his 1973
novella *Xala*
Production Companies
Filmi Doomireew
(Films Domirev)
Société Nationale de
Cinéma
Production Manager
Paulin Soumanou Vieyra
Director of Photography
Georges Caristan
Assistant Camera
Orlando L. López
Seydina D. Saye
Farba Seck
Editor
Florence Eymon
Set Photographer
Michel Renaudeau
Production Secretary
Carrie D. Sembene
Props
Doudou Guèye
Lighting
Émile Ganem
Chérif Dia
Dofonou E. Lazare
Production Managers
Ababacar Samb
Ibrahima Barro

Sound
El Hadji M'Bow
Mawa Gaye
Original Music
Samba Diabaré Samb
Original Lyrics
Ousmane Sembene
Trainees
Eva Feigeles
Catherine Quesmand

CAST
(NB: the opening credits
are limited and names
are not matched with
a character, so the
list of roles remains
incomplete)
Thierno Lèye
El Hadji Abdou Kader
Bèye
Douta Seck
Gorgui Bèye
Seune Samb
Adja Awa Astou,
El Hadji's first wife
Dyella Touré
N'Goné, El Hadji's
third wife
Younousse Sèye
Oumi N'Doye, El Hadji's
second wife
Myriam Niang
Rama Bèye, El Hadji's
daughter
Ilimane Sagna
Modu, El Hadji's
chauffeur

Magaye Niang
Monsieur Thieli,
the pickpocket
Fatim Diagne
Madame Diouf, El Hadji's
secretary
Dieynaba Niang
Yay Bineta, the *badiène*
Farba Sarr
the 'cuz' (banking
official)
Moustapha Touré
Ahmed Fall
Martin Sow
Sérigne Mada
Makhourédia Guèye
Président of the Chamber
Abdoulaye Seck
Kebe, the deputy
Mamadou Sarr
Chamber member
Paul-André Pellegrin
Jean-Paul Salaün
Marcel Beziau
European advisors
(including Monsieur
Dupont-Durand)
Star Band de Dakar
as themselves

uncredited
Langouste Drobe
Abdoulaye Boye
Papa Oumar Diop
Papa Demba Diallo

Production Details

Original French title:
L'Impuissance sexuelle
temporaire
French and Wolof with
English subtitles
35mm
1.66:1
Colour (Eastmancolor)
Mono
Running time:
123 minutes
(NB: The DVD version
by New Yorker Films is
precisely 122 minutes,
52 seconds, while that
by Capuseen [France] is
117 minutes, 57 seconds)

Release Details

Premièred at the Moscow
Film Festival in July 1975
and released with cuts
in Senegal in 1975.
US theatrical release
in October 1975 by
New Yorker Films
UK theatrical release
in 1976 by Contemporary
Films